THINGS
THAT
LAST

THINGS THAT LAST

Reflections on
Faith, Hope, and Love

RUBEL SHELLY

HOWARD
PUBLISHING CO.

3117 North 7th
West Monroe, Louisiana 71291

The purpose of Howard Publishing is threefold:

*Inspiring holiness in the lives of believers,

*Instilling hope in the hearts of struggling people
everywhere,

*Instructing believers toward a deeper faith in Jesus Christ,

Because he's coming again.

Howard Publishers
3117 North 7th Street, West Monroe, LA 71291-2227

Printed in the United States of America

First Printing 1991

ISBN# 1-878990-19-5

Table of Contents

Section One: Faith

Section Two: Hope

Section Three: Love

Section One

Faith

"Your Daddy Must Be Crazy!"

What would you do if you were a high school football player whose coach sent in a play which called for you to run the ball to your *opponent's* goal line? It has happened!

With seven seconds left in the game, Tishimingo High School was leading Falkner High School, 16-14. At stake was a berth in Mississippi's 1988 state class 1A playoffs. Tishimingo had the ball on Falkner's 40-yard line. All they had to do was run out the clock on the next play, and they would win the game by two points.

Coach David Herbert, who has Lou Gehrig's disease and coaches from a seat in the back of a pickup truck, sent in a play to his son and the team's quarterback, Dave Herbert. The play called for a handoff to tailback Shane Hill and for him to run as fast as he could for Falkner's goal line.

"Your daddy must be crazy!" protested one of the tackles. So, while the argument went on in the team's huddle, a delay-of-game penalty was called on Tishimingo. Finally the team lined up, the ball was handed off to the tailback, and he ran 55 yards in the "wrong" direction. He laid down in the opponent's end zone and waited for the clock to expire with practically everyone on the field and in the stadium bewildered. A two-point safety for Falkner. Score tied. Time expired.

Was the coach crazy? Like a fox, maybe. You see, in order for his team to reach the playoffs, Tishimingo had to beat Falkner by four or more points. After thinking about the chances of going 40 yards on one play or kicking a field goal from that distance, he decided overtime was his best bet. Thus the strategy which appeared so muddleheaded.

"The message of the cross is foolishness to those who are perishing. . ."

Had the tailback been chased down and tackled, Falkner would have suffered a two-point loss but would have gone to the playoffs. But not one of its players gave chase to the ball carrier.

What was the result of the maneuver? Tishimingo won in overtime, 22-16, on a third-down, two-yard run by Shane Hill. Hill finished the game with minus 29 yards for the night. But his team won and went to the playoffs.

Sounds a bit like the cross to me. God became a man, was pushed around by his enemies, and was executed as a criminal by the Roman procurator of Palestine. Satan appeared to have won. Jesus of Nazareth was dead. His disciples were scattered. God had suffered defeat. Or had he?

Three days later, Jesus was alive from the dead. Over a period of 40 days, he showed himself alive to hundreds of people. Then, 51 days later, Peter explained that it had all been part of a divine strategy. He said, "This man was handed over to you by God's set purpose and foreknowledge" (Acts 2:23). He continued and cited Old Testament predictions which had been fulfilled by the resurrection. The crescendo came when he announced: "God has made this Jesus, whom you crucified, both Lord and Christ" (Acts 2:36b).

There you have it! A game plan that looked to all the world like craziness. One which still confounds disciples in our church-huddles and observers in the world-stadium alike. But the Son executed his Father's call to perfection. He died on the cross to pay the sin debt of the human race.

"For the message of the cross is foolishness to those who are perishing, but to us who are being saved it is the power of God" (1 Cor. 1:18).

Two thousand years this side of the event, we still proclaim that foolishness to be the wisdom and power of God.

Unsure About
Your Pardon?

It was one of those headlines sure to catch my eye: *"Hearst Shaw Unsure Pardon Coming."* The story ran in newspapers around the country on January 18, 1989. Two days before the end of Ronald Reagan's second term.

Patty Hearst Shaw was convicted for her role in a 1974 bank robbery and served 23 months in prison. She has maintained all along that she had been brainwashed by a group of self-styled "revolutionaries" who kidnapped her, terrorized her, and temporarily took away her power to make free choices.

Toward the end of any presidential term, names are brought to the Chief Executive's attention for possible pardon. In August of 1988, Shaw requested a pardon for the bank hold-up. And recently President Reagan had expressed an interest in her petition.

The anxiety must have been tremendous for her. Will he remember my appeal? Will he take action on it? When will I know something?

Although several pardons were granted and signed during the final days of Mr. Reagan's term as president, the Shaw pardon was not forthcoming. So the request which had given way to anxiety eventually ended in disappointment.

Christians have a better expectation. Wanting a pardon, there is no misgiving about its availability. Needing the burden of the past removed, there is absolute assurance of God's willingness to purge your record. The Son of God has been presented "as a sacrifice of atonement" so that all of us may be "justified freely by God's grace through the redemption that came by Christ Jesus" (Rom. 3:24).

Christians have a better expectation. Wanting a pardon, there is no misgiving about its availability.

When a penitent sinner submits to the rite of baptism in Jesus' name, the cleansing of sin's guilt by Christ's blood is symbolized to him by the bathing of his body in water. For that person, baptism becomes "not the removal of dirt from the body but the pledge of a good conscience toward God" (1 Pet. 3:21). It seals, validates, and affirms *pardon*. It is a washing of regeneration (Tit. 3:5). A new birth of water and the Spirit (John 3:5).

Past the point of receiving your pardon, rejoice, breathe freely, and enjoy the life of a free person in Christ.

"Therefore, there is now no condemnation for those who are in Christ Jesus" (Rom. 8:1). The occasional Christian who lives with a parolee mentality (i.e., anxious, burdened with remorse, trying to appease God with guilt-inspired works, afraid of God) betrays a lack of confidence in God's promise of pardon.

Patty Hearst Shaw's *presidential* pardon didn't come. My *divine* pardon has. And so has yours. Instead of headlining our lives with guilt and uncertainty, then, we can celebrate the ecstasy of pardon. The gift of grace. The freedom of forgiveness.

Things That
Make People Laugh

It's interesting to study what makes a person laugh. Sometimes it is a revealing bit of research. Sometimes it even contains spiritual insight.

Most of our attempts at humor are rather innocuous. Take the light-bulb jokes which first appeared in the 1960s. They originally tended to target Polish people, but no group has been spared them since that time:

How many New Yorkers does it take to change a light bulb? Three. One to screw it in and two to criticize.

How many Californians does it take to change a light bulb? Ten. One to screw it in and nine to share the experience.

How many psychiatrists does it take to change a light bulb? Only one, but the light bulb really has to want to change.

How many preachers does it take to change a light bulb? Only one, but he will thunder "Let there be light" just before the final twist of his wrist and take a collection when he has finished.

Ethnic jokes may often be less than innocent and can serve to promote stereotypes and prejudice. The English joke about the Irish, whites about blacks, males about females, etc. The jokes that some people find "sidesplitters" are to others "sick."

But laughter sometimes has a stimulus other than a joke. Take Sarah's laughter as a case in point (Gen. 18:1-15). The Lord appeared to her husband Abraham and said, "I will surely return to you about this time next year, and Sarah your wife will have a son." She overheard the conversation and "laughed to herself" at the thought of having a child at her age. When confronted about her laughter, "she lied and said, `I did not laugh.' " (What most of us tend to forget is that Abraham himself had the same response to the notion of being a father when he first heard it. Gen. 17:17.)

This is the *laughter of unbelief.* The chuckling of incredulity. The snickering of skepticism.

Contrary to one's first-blush reaction, this sort of laughter is not sinister in tone. It doesn't betray hardness of heart or rebellion against God. It more often signifies that one has heard about or has been offered something that is judged too good to be true.

Think how you'd react if someone called to say you had just won the Publisher's Clearinghouse Sweepstakes. You would probably think some friend was playing a prank and respond with a giggled "Sure, and I've been drafted by the Demopublican Party to run for president." Isn't that the natural understanding of what happened when Abraham and Sarah first heard the news of a son? They couldn't believe that what they had wanted for decades was finally going to happen.

Here are some situations we sometimes receive with mock laughter. Not because we are wicked. But because they hold out such wonderful prospects to us that we have a hard time believing it could be true.

The promise of forgiveness. Evelyn was a Christian lady who had been unfaithful to her husband of nine years, gotten pregnant, and had an abortion. Four months later, she was telling me about it. Confessing it for the first time. Wanting guidance.

We talked for over an hour. She loved her husband. She had just been vulnerable at a time when they had been having some problems. The other man came along and paid her attention, to use Evelyn's words, "at just the wrong time." They had a three-week affair. She discovered she was pregnant. And she did the only thing her panicked soul could think of to hide her sin. Now she was paying a double debt to guilt.

At the end of that session, we prayed. She asked to be forgiven. I prayed for God to heal her soul and to strengthen her marriage. When we opened our eyes and looked at each other, I said, "You're forgiven. Do you believe that?" She laughed. Not a mean, mocking laugh. A shy, doubting laugh. Her laugh was akin to Sarah's. It said she hadn't been whipped, exposed to public ridicule, or stoned. It said that she thought it had been too easy.

Just one talk and a prayer. So we talked a while longer about the price of our pardon.

Forgiveness *isn't* easy, and grace *doesn't* come cheaply. But God assumed our debt and paid our penalty at Calvary. Now our genuine sorrow over our personal sins gives us access to Christ's blood. To forgiveness. To new beginnings. And Evelyn sobbed again. This time it was the sobbing of relief. She understood and believed that she was forgiven. Years after the fact, she is living joyously in the Lord and with her husband.

Some things make us laugh because they hold such wonderful prospects that it is hard to believe they are true.

The prospect of change. You likely remember the response of the Christians in Jerusalem when Saul of Tarsus returned there after his conversion. Dr. Luke tells us that "they were all afraid of him, not believing that he really was a disciple" (Acts 9:26). In effect, they laughed off the possibility that anyone could change so drastically from the man they knew Saul had been.

We still do the same thing occasionally. We think that someone either can't or hasn't changed, so we refuse to allow her to exhibit change. At other times we explore every sort of option for effecting change in situations without turning to the Lord as the principal agent of change in human lives. Preachers, counselors, programs, and books may *assist* with change, but genuine and lasting change in human character comes by the Spirit of God.

More often than despairing of change in others, however, is the anguish of heart one feels over his own perceived inability to change. To be victorious over a temptation. To ride out and overcome a grief or loss. To break a crippling addiction.

At the age of 63, Arnold had been an alcoholic all his adult life. He had functioned. He had hidden his slavery from all but a handful of people. They had covered up for him, lied for him, and protected him from the consequences of his drinking. Now that he was retired, however, he was drinking more than ever. He was killing himself. When his family finally confronted him about his alcoholism and his wife told him she was leaving unless he got help, he laughed. I was sitting right beside him but would have heard the laugh in the next room.

It was a doleful and sorrowful laugh. He wanted help but didn't know any was available. He wanted to be well but thought it was impossible. He had long known that he wanted to stop drinking but had discovered that willpower and grim determination were not enough.

But Arnold is a Christian and believes in the power of God to change both things and people. He knows that the power at work in the people of God is greater than the power at work in the world. He just didn't know how to tap into that power for his particular problem. He went into treatment, admitted his powerlessness over alcohol, and surrendered himself to God. He turned his addictive behavior over to God for solution rather than continue his self-willed, self-destructive drinking.

Today he is not only sober but enjoying life. He has conversations and remembers them. He plays with his grandchildren, and they enjoy being with him. God is giving him a day-by-day victory over something he thought was impossible to change.

A call to accomplish. Moses had been in the desert for 40 years, a fugitive from Egyptian justice, when God appeared to him in the burning-bush episode. He called Moses to become the deliverer of Israel.

The response Moses made probably included laughter. Read his words with laughter in your voice, and you know that inflection represents his feelings: "Who am I, that I should go to Pharaoh and bring the Israelites out of Egypt?" (Ex. 3:11).

Our God has a history of doing unheard-of things. So try not to laugh, and believe instead.

So God argued with Moses. He answered his quibbles and misgivings about dealing with the ruler of Egypt. He promised him the presence of miraculous signs to demonstrate to Pharaoh his divine commission. He sent his brother Aaron along with him to handle some of the public speaking. He said, "I will help both of you speak and will teach you what to do" (Ex. 4:15b).

People are still reluctant to accept the calls of opportunity God puts before them. Whether from false modesty or true fear, they depreciate their ability to cope with challenge. They sell themselves short. They forget that the power sufficient to the task will be provided by the one who called them to it.

The call doesn't have to be monumental to be from God. You don't have to see a burning bush or have the fate of the whole world in your hands. "But in fact God has arranged the parts in the body, every one of them, just as he wanted them to be" (1 Cor. 12:18). Your present challenge is appropriate both to your faith and to your growth. Accept it, and trust God to work all things for good in the situation.

The laughter which comes of a healthy sense of humor is a good thing. Of this sort of laughter, the Bible says: "A cheerful heart is good medicine" (Prov.17:22a). It keeps us from taking life in general and ourselves in particular too seriously. So the next time you have a good laugh, thank God for the opportunity.

But try not to laugh at the wrong time. Resist the temptation to laugh with incredulity. Believe the outrageous promises God has made to you. Trust him to forgive, change, and work through you. Don't give way to unbelief. Don't mock God's mercy.

Our God has a history of doing unheard-of things. Instead of laughing, then, trust, "for it is God who works in you to will and to act according to his good purpose" (Phil. 2:13).

When Issues
Aren't Issues

From all the attention given to it, you'd have thought there was something ultimately significant about the clothing styles and fingernails of Florence Griffith-Joyner.

Judging by the amount of press it received, you might have been fooled into thinking there was something truly important about who got locked out of the building at the 1988 Democratic National Convention or how many balloons there were in the Bush demonstration at the Republican National Convention. Newscasters talked at great length about both.

And someone could mistakenly conclude that it matters in some critical sense whether Jesus returns in September 1997 or May 2412. People are always writing books which claim to have discovered the key to interpreting God's timetable for the end of the world.

We human beings have a terrible tendency for confusing the marginal with the momentous, the petty with the profound, the worthless with the weighty. So we wind up living with inverted priorities. Majoring in minors. Missing the point of it all.

The *real* issue about Florence Griffith-Joyner was not her exotic running suits and long fingernails but her dazzling speed as a sprinter in the 100- and 200-meter dash. She won the 100-meters, set a world record of 21.34 seconds in the 200, and ran on the United States gold-medal 400-meter relay team at the 1988 summer Olympics.

The *real* issue in Atlanta and New Orleans was whether or not the democratic process could work to find, nominate, and elect a president who can lead the most powerful nation in the world.

We confuse worthless and weighty. Major in minors. Miss the point of it all.

And the *real* issue about the second coming of Christ is simply that he *is* coming to judge the world in righteousness, and we must be ready to meet him at any moment.

Nobody has been worse over the centuries about confusing inconsequential topics with ponderous ones than religious people. Debating details of what constituted a violation of the sabbath, some people failed to use the day for meaningful worship. Disagreeing about how many angels could dance on the head of a pin, theologians have let people die of starvation in the shadow of their cathedrals. While disputing the relative merits of Bible translations, we have let people die without any knowledge of the Word of God.

In other words, we have tended to confuse *issues* with *incidentals*. Running suits with running skill. Auditoriums with what happens in them. Foolhardy attempts at date-setting for serious preparation against the Day of the Lord.

Jesus had a funny metaphor for this sort of thing: *straining out gnats and swallowing camels!*

I'm glad he lets us laugh at ourselves about it. It seems far more natural to cry. In either case, the point is to be warned against ceaseless repetition of this foolish tendency. When you insist on making something an issue in your own mind, between you and a friend, or before God, make sure it really deserves the status.

Bone-Headed Questions

Asking questions is a good thing to do. Albert Einstein once said: "Curiosity has its own reason for existence. Never lose a holy curiosity."

What he called "holy curiosity" is healthy. It promotes scientific discovery. It is at the heart of a good education. It generates spiritual growth. People who fear honest questions are too insecure to be trusted.

But sometimes we jeopardize getting the insights we need because of asking the *wrong* questions. Even stupid questions. Or, as my Dad called them, "bone-headed questions." Those questions can give away our total ignorance on the subject at hand. They would make it difficult for even an Einstein to help us. No, even for Jesus to help us.

Take these examples of misguided questions which were put to Jesus. They'll help you understand the truth that some questions poison the well of learning.

"Lord, how many times shall I forgive my brother when he sins against me? Up to seven times?"

"Why do you eat with tax collectors and sinners?"

"There are six days for work. Why did you heal this crippled woman on the sabbath day?"

Good questions generate growth. Bone-headed questions make it difficult to understand God's will.

Do you see the point now? Peter's question implied a predetermined limit to forgiveness; Jesus' answer was that he should forgive without keeping count. The Pharisees' question assumed that good people avoided bad people; Jesus' answer affirmed that God's people seek out lost ones to bring them the news of salvation. The critics of his sabbath healing raised a question which displayed wooden literalism with Scripture and stone-heartedness toward people; Jesus responded by affirming that the intent of divine law was ever and only to affirm God's love for human beings rather than to deepen their misery.

We still ask some pretty dim-witted questions. Take these as examples:

"Do you let divorced people (alcoholics, people with AIDS, folks with prison records, etc.) come to your church?"

"I'm sure God has a purpose for it. Why do you think he took Kathy's baby (sight, health, etc.) from her?"

"I know he's really sorry. How long should I let him `stew in his juices' before making peace with him?"

Yes sir, the age of miracles may have passed. But the age of dumb questions hasn't!

(Note: Supply your own answers to the questions above. To check them, compare your answers to the content and tone of Jesus' answers already cited.)

Some Things Are Etched in Stone

It is called simply "The Wall." It is our nation's monument to American soldiers who died in Vietnam. Located in Washington D. C., it is somber-looking black granite which lists 58,132 names of people who made the supreme sacrifice in service to the USA.

An eerie thing happened in November of 1987. Darrall E. Lausch learned that his name has been engraved on the wall since its erection in 1982. Lausch, a farmer and part-time construction worker, is very much alive and well. He is the third living veteran whose name has been found to be incorrectly included on a monument to the dead.

Lausch's attitude about it? "Anybody can make a mistake, even the system," he said. And the Vietnam Veterans Memorial Foundation's attitude toward the problem? The mistake is incorrectable, unfortunately, for it is "etched in stone." A *faux pas* is permanently in place.

Life can do the same cruel thing in a variety of ways. And some of them are more significant, painful, and personal than having one's name entered incorrectly or misspelled or otherwise abused.

Len Bias was a 6-foot-8 All-American at the University of Maryland. In the spring of 1986, he was at the top of the world of athletics. He was drafted by the NBA's Boston Celtics June 17; he signed a multimillion-dollar contract with Reebok shoes June 18; he died of cardiac arrhythmia after snorting cocaine June 19. Drug habit? One-time "celebration"? Nobody knows for sure, and it doesn't really matter. His needless, pointless death stands etched in stone.

Mathias Rust is a 19-year-old West German who thought it would be a neat bit of mischief to fly his tiny Cessna 172 over the border of the Soviet Union and land in Red Square. He would even deliver a peace message to the amused Kremlin leaders. The immature young man found out that the Russian sense of humor is different from that of Westerners. Cute prank? Slap on the wrist? Hardly! Rust had to serve several months in a Soviet labor camp for his miscalculation. His arrest and punishment etched his mistake in stone.

Doug Mansfield was an A student who played football for Humboldt (Tenn.) High School. A "good boy" and "quiet kid" who was not known for outbursts of temper, he played nose guard in the 1987 Class AA state playoff game. Upset over his team's 14-13 loss in the game's final two minutes, he pulled on his helmet again after the game was over, sprinted several feet, and butted his head against a brick wall outside the dressing room.

The impact broke his neck, severed his spinal cord, and left him paralyzed. A stupid stunt has been etched in stone for a high school senior.

They're just kids. It doesn't seem right for them to suffer such horrendous consequences for such immature things. But life is unyielding. The pragmatic reason any of us should be cautious or take care about the things we do is that consequences are real. Automobiles are dangerous. Drugs and alcohol can ruin lives and kill people. "Innocent flirtations" can break up marriages. A one-night stand with a stranger can infect someone with gonorrhea or AIDS. Sowing wild oats can reap a bumper crop of pain and regret.

The pragmatic reason for taking care about things we do is that consequences are real.

I hate to lay a bummer on you. It's much more to my liking to be upbeat and positive. In fact, some people say that the positives are all they are willing to hear. But maybe those are the people who don't take life seriously enough. You don't have to be a drag to have an occasional serious thought, wear a coat in cold weather, or realize how dangerous it is to skate on spiritually thin ice.

Yes, I know that some settings call for quick courage. There is sometimes a need to be bold, daring, and a risk-taker. Abraham moved from the security of Ur to an unknown future. Moses took on the leadership of two million people for a desert crossing. The apostles left family, careers, and their former concepts of God to walk with Jesus into an uncertain mission. These people took risks for the sake of their faith. They changed the course of the world by daring to do bold things. But that sort of boldness is very different from the foolish, short-sighted, dangerous things we sometimes do.

Remember Esau? He traded away his inheritance rights for a single meal! "Afterward, as you know, when he wanted to inherit this blessing, he was rejected. He could bring about no change of mind, though he sought the blessing with tears" (Heb. 12:17). The foolish choice he made that day had been etched in stone, and the regret he felt for years and years afterward changed nothing.

So be bold for the sake of doing right. Be courageous to follow the Lord in spite of obstacles or discouragements. Be daring enough to take the risks that are necessary to make spiritual changes for the better in your own life or to accomplish something which has the potential to bless the lives of others.

But don't trade tomorrow's health and well-being for today's trendy dare. Don't sacrifice forever on the altar of immediacy. Don't do something stupid that will cripple you physically, emotionally, or spiritually for life. Don't think for a minute that only other people have to pay for their follies.

Maybe you've gotten away with some cliffhangers before. What could have been major disaster for any one of us has slid by to leave hardly a scratch. But against that sort of foolish risk-taking as a way of life, somebody needs to remind us occasionally that mistakes are sometimes engraved as a permanent record.

Courage to take risks when it is necessary. Wisdom to flee when the risks are foolish ones. God, grant us the discernment to know the difference between the two, lest we spend the rest of our lives staring at *mistakes which have been etched in stone.*

Life on a Tiny Pond

Maybe you're familiar with Carmen de Gasztold's "Prayer of the Little Ducks." I ran across it for the first time a while back.

> *Dear God,*
> *give us a flood of water.*
> *Let it rain tomorrow and always.*
> *Give us plenty of little slugs*
> *and other luscious things to eat.*
> *Protect all folk who quack*
> *and everyone who knows how to*
> *swim. Amen.*

Don't we all tend to live with just that narrow a perspective on life? Oh, for the purpose of gathering and processing information, I am the center of my *perceptual* universe. But I am not the center of *the* universe.

A boy who grows up in a town of less than 500 people has no idea of Nashville, New York, or Africa. A teacher or book may introduce such places, but he has to go there to sense how small and narrow his world has been before. At first he is frightened, for things are so different. Then he begins to be excited about new horizons and open to discovery.

What is true of geography is even truer of intellectual horizons. So long as one swims only in a little pond, the delights of stream, river, and ocean are unreal to her. In the initial visits, there may be fear. Ideally, though, she comes to revel in the thrill of discovering new ideas and experiencing the things those new ideas open to her.

And Jesus came to break the shackles which arise from living in too narrow a spiritual world.

You can rise above your fears.
You can revel in discovery.
You can experience new things.

So he said the most important thing is to love God with your whole being. God is creator, and you are creature. The true and ultimate meaning of your life is found in him and his will. To lose your life in his is to find life; to stay in your little pond of self-interest is to miss life.

The second most important thing is to love your neighbor as you love yourself. Escaping your little duck pond of selfishness, see abused children, homeless women, drunken men. See unemployed adults and confused teens.

See the lost and the dying. Then, once you have seen them, *care* that they are as they are. Do something to help one of them. A cup of water. A sweater. A pat on the back or a hug. Doing it to one of them is doing it to Jesus.

We are all limited by factors beyond our control. A white southern American with a high school education sees the world differently from a black mid-western American who has an M.A. in economics. Both of them see it differently from a Russian or Brazilian or Kenyan. Reality is larger than any of us, and it is only egocentric illusion that allows one of us to think that his perspective disallows all others.

And think of the ink and blood which have been spilled needlessly both in human relationships and in theology. A woman will not see her friend's point of view. A husband will not hear his wife's opinion. A dogmatic believer disrupts the unity of the church over a cherished belief that his understanding of how to go about the project is correct above all others.

The tragedy of a narrow view is a bounded, self-absorbed, dull life in a tiny pond. The ducks in that pond may be blissfully happy in their ignorance for a time. After a while, however, they notice visitors to their pond who smile at them and talk about how cute they are. But those visitors hardly ever want to swim in their water. They even notice the scummy surface that tends to form in stagnant waters. But they are used to it and can live with it.

More and more they begin to miss young ducklings who leave the pond and never return, but they put it down to "duckling disease" and seem to recall that those ducklings were never really very healthy looking anyway.

The pond is typically quiet. Oh, occasionally a couple of older ducks will get into quacking contests, take a few pecks at each other, and swim henceforth with their backs toward each other and with their wilted tail feathers as high as they can carry them.

So they swim. Thinking that theirs is the only pond in the cosmos. Praying for rain. Praying for little slugs. Praying for all folk who quack and everyone who knows how to swim. Sadly unaware of fresh streams, sunny beaches, happy people, or the God who created them all.

Stretch the envelope of your world. Read. Get to know people from backgrounds different from your own. Travel to places you have only heard about but think it would be fun to see for yourself.

Rather than be threatened by people with a different point of view from your own, learn from them. Try to figure out how the person came to that conviction. Look for some underlying assumption or belief which accounts for the opposing views you have. Express your own opinion with charm rather than venom. Learn to respect people who differ with you. If you see something you never saw before and change your mind on a point, be honest enough to admit it.

Life is meant to be a high-seas adventure. What a waste it would be for you to *duck* the challenge and let its excitement pass you by like water running off a *you-know-what's* back.

Where Questions Are Answered

An important part of living is learning to ask questions. The *right* questions. Then you must know where to go to find answers. *Correct* answers.

I'm not talking about trivial questions such as "What must I do to be rich and famous?" Nor evil questions like "How can I get even with her?" Not even important practical questions such as "Should we buy a house?" or "How can we afford to send our son to college?" The questions I have in mind are the ones which deal with themes from the Word of God. Questions about spiritual issues.

Although some of us were reared in the tradition of going to the Bible for answers, we may have missed the point of why Scripture exists. First, we sometimes take the wrong questions to the Word of God. Second, with the wrong list of questions in hand, we almost surely miss the ultimate answer found there.

Here, for example, are some of the wrong questions we carry to Scripture: Where is the proof for my position? Where is the justification for my prejudice? Where is the biblical club with which I can bash my opponent in argument? With a list like this in hand, one does strange things with the Word of God. Things happen in the name of God that were never meant to happen. He does not bless them. They do not prosper.

An important part of living is learning to ask questions. The *right* questions.

It might be a worthwhile thing to go from Genesis through Revelation marking questions with a highlighter. I've never taken the time to do that, but I did thumb through to jot down a few of the ones which stand out in bold letters over time:

Am I my brother's keeper?

If a man dies, will he live again?

What good will it be for a man if he gains the whole world, yet forfeits his soul? Or what can a man give in exchange for his soul?

Sirs, what must I do to be saved?

What a wretched man I am! Who will rescue me from this body of death?

Who will bring any charge against those whom God has chosen? . . . Who shall separate us from the love of Christ?

You can probably enlarge the list from your own knowledge of the Word of God. As a matter of fact, you can probably recast each of these biblical questions into your own words by recalling words which have come from your mouth during the last week: *What am I going to do? How can I cope with this? What is happening to my family? Where do I turn for help?*

There is a place where all these questions, and any others worth being asked, are answered. There they are given a single, definitive, final answer. Any question not answered there is trivial, and any answer other than the one found there is incomplete at best.

All our questions are answered by virtue of a cross and the one who died on it 2,000 years ago.

If you cannot love your brother whom you have seen, you cannot love God whom you have not seen.

He is not here. He is risen! . . . Christ has indeed been raised from the dead, the firstfruits of those who have fallen asleep.

Do not put your hope in wealth, which is so uncertain, but put your hope in God.

Believe in the Lord Jesus Christ, and you will be saved, you and your household. . . . Repent and be baptized, every one of you, in the name of Jesus Christ so that your sins may be forgiven.

Thanks be to God, through Jesus Christ our Lord! . . . Therefore, there is now no condemnation for those who are in Christ Jesus.

Nothing in all creation will be able to separate us from the love of God that is in Christ Jesus our Lord.

There you have it. One event responds to our human need. A single circumstance answers all the questions. It doesn't take a genius to see that the answers given above to the questions which began this essay are made possible by means of the death of Jesus.

Is today's church in search of a "relevant" message? Then let's have fewer seminars on "Aerobics for Jesus" and more on the meaning of the cross. Let's spend less of our time with trivial sermons and classes on such issues as "Should Christians Swim at Public Beaches?" or "Which Version of the Bible Shall We Read?" and give more time to serious examination of the text of Scripture.

Want to know why young people are abandoning churches in droves for the New Age Movement? Their churches are into frivolous and lightweight topics, but they want to ask fundamental questions about human life.

The trend will not be reversed until we revive the issue of Jesus and focus everything on his cross. The cross must be more than a mere symbol.

We'll call him Robert. He had preached for four churches over a period of 17 years. He had been invited to speak at several "major events" of the sorts that massage preachers' egos. He had written a few articles which had been published in religious journals.

Robert is a fire-breather. He points his finger. He names names. He announces God's judgment without hesitation on smokers, dancers, and swimmers. He knows how long a girl's shorts must be and how long a boy's hair ought to be. He explains grace in terms of what one must do to have it. A theological liberal is anyone who doesn't accept all of his dogmatic conclusions.

Robert was recently found out for his latest in a series of affairs with women where he has preached. His wife is divorcing him. His life is a shambles.

Maybe now Robert can discover what his ministry should have been built around for the past 17 years. Maybe his focus will shift from harsh judgment to joyous gospel. In my last conversation with him, it seemed apparent that his issues of concern were different. Deeper. Christ-centered rather than crowd-pleasing. Spiritual rather than carnal.

What a shame that he misspent 17 years and had to discover his Savior in the shambles of his ministry. What heartache there is in the fact that the people who listened and believed what he had taught during those 17 years have no place for him now and can only judge and reject him.

The cross is wiser than our wisdom, more powerful than our strength. All that is ultimate is found there. Maybe, then, we should all rethink our lists of questions. We must come to the point of disaffection with the answers we can find through our searchings and rejoice in the single answer that has been given us at Calvary.

Living Beneath Yourself

Perhaps you saw the sad picture and read the astonishing article which appeared with it in newspapers across the country.

Victor Fimia was shown leaning against his jail cell in Santa Rosa, California. He had been arrested for panhandling and public drunkenness. Unable to pay his $50 bail, he was resigned to serving out his time in the Somona County Jail. A self-described "wino" at age 40, a stubby beard, a missing tooth, and shabby clothes gave him the appearance of a typical down-and-outer.

The fact of the matter is, however, that Victor Fimia was a wealthy man who didn't know of his good fortune. He has been sleeping in an old sleeping bag and getting meals wherever he could find them for the past 23 years. Through a police computer check after his arrest, it was learned that his family reported him missing from San Jose years ago. His father died about five years ago and left him an inheritance of some $30,000 to $40,000.

For all that time, a man has done without, suffered needlessly, and lived as a pauper for no good reason.

It reminds me of the way many of us live who are children of God. We live in horrible circumstances for no good reason. Though heirs of God and fellow heirs with Jesus Christ (Rom. 8:17), we are living as spiritual paupers.

Though forgiven of every sin by the blood of Christ, some of us keep tormenting ourselves for things which happened long ago. "As far as east is from the west, so far does he remove our transgressions from us" (Psa. 103:12).

Though promised his strength in our times of weakness and stress, many of us keep trying to cope with life in our own unaided power. Thus we continue to fail. "Cast all your anxieties on him, for he cares about you" (1 Pet. 5:7).

Too many children of God live in horrible circumstances for no good reason.

Though having access to the boundless resources of God through prayer, most of us are "too busy" to pray, falling on our knees only when we "don't know what else to do." "And this is the confidence which we have in him, that if we ask anything according to his will he hears us" (1 John 5:14).

Though assured of victory over sin and a home in heaven, it appears that doubt and frustration rule the lives of many believers. "[Nothing] in all creation will be able to separate us from the love of God in Christ Jesus our Lord" (Rom. 8:39).

Victor Fimia had been living an undesirable and unenviable life for years. He had been living beneath himself. So what did he plan to do when his wealth arrived? He said he would "go down to the liquor store to finish my bottle of wine."

The story sounds more like Christians all the time. Even though we know we generally live beneath our redeemed selves, we keep returning to the futile things of this life. It need not be so. We can live as children of a King.

You Shall Know
the Truth . . .

Jesus Christ is truth personified. His *words* are the truth on whatever issue he addresses. His *behavior* is truth exemplified. Put most simply, he *is* the truth.

Because of our Lord's relationship to the matter, one would naturally expect truth to be a key issue with his disciples. Jesus indicated as much on several occasions. He wants all who follow him to love, seek, and live the truth. Life and sanctification are in the truth.

The subject isn't simply important, then, but essential and indispensable. So think about what Jesus said, and could have said, about our ability to know the truth.

You shall know the truth, but the truth will be hard for you to hear.

All of us bring our personal histories to every encounter with truth. Everything that is part of our diverse backgrounds colors, prejudices, and blinds us. I can sometimes see the truth about you so much easier than you can, and you often see me far more perceptively than I can see myself.

You shall know the truth, but the truth will first make you miserable.

Receiving truth requires an honesty and humility which some can never achieve. They are happier in self-deception than in the truth, for truth confronts everything that is shallow and false in a person. That confrontation is so painful for some that they will perpetuate lies and dishonesty rather than accept the truth about themselves.

You shall know the truth, but it will be painful to do something about it.

Receiving the truth requires an honesty and humilty which some can never achieve.

Fact-truths (e.g., "My car was stolen" or "I was wrong about that") are hard enough, but relationship-truths (e.g., "Your baby is dying" or "I broke her heart" or "I disobeyed God") are much harder still. These truths almost always mean that somebody needs to do something, change, or repent. And change can be very painful.

You shall know the truth, and the truth will set you free.

Ah, that's the beauty of truth. For all the difficulty of hearing, accepting, or acting on the truth, its value is vindicated in the outcome. The humble, teachable heart can be set free of sin and enslavement. It can be liberated from fear and dishonor. It can be delivered from evil and stand in the light.

Truth challenges. Truth often hurts. Truth makes tough, unyielding demands. But if anyone would enter into life, truth is the door through which he must pass.

The Man at the Controls

Captain David M. Cronin was piloting United Airlines Flight 811 from Honolulu to Auckland, New Zealand, on February 24, 1989. The Boeing 747 had just topped 22,000 feet. Passing through some thunderstorms, everything appeared unremarkable and routine.

Suddenly there was a tremendous decompression explosion as an 11-by-20-foot opening was ripped into the right side of the plane. Apparently a cargo door had not been closed properly, or a latch on the door was faulty. Nine people were sucked from the jumbo jet to their deaths over the Pacific Ocean.

Captain Cronin, due to take mandatory retirement at age 60 on March 23, managed to get the wounded bird back to Honolulu during 18 minutes which must have seemed like an eternity. Using everything he knew from 38 years of flying, he dealt with the loss of two of his four engines, a stuck right wing flap, and a huge hole in the side of the plane which sent tornado-like winds through the fuselage and made it shake violently. Three hundred and forty-five passengers and crew members praised him for making the right decisions and handling the circumstance heroically. The plane's landing was gentle and took only two-thirds of the runway.

When there is a crisis which has already killed some and threatens to kill everyone else on board, you want the right person at the controls of a jumbo jet. And at the controls of the universe.

When a crisis has already killed some and threatens to kill everyone else on board, you want the right person at the controls.

The Person. Jesus Christ is the one who created this universe aeons ago and who maintains it yet by his power. "Through him all things were made; without him nothing was made that has been made" (John 1:3). "For by him all things were created: things in heaven and on earth, visible and invisible, whether thrones or powers or rulers or authorities; all things were created by him and for him. He is before all things, and in him all things hold together" (Col. 1:16-17). "The Son is the radiance of God's glory and the exact representation of his being, sustaining all things by his powerful word" (Heb. 1:3).

That he created and steers this cosmos of ours is not to say that he is responsible for everything that goes on in it. Earth is not only subject to accidental disasters but is fatally flawed because of the sin its passengers have introduced into its inner workings.

In spite of the horrors of sin, the loss of some already to death, and the peril to the remainder of us, God the Son has never abandoned his creation. He still loves us with an everlasting love. It is not his will that a single one of us should perish. And, yes, he is still at the controls of this crippled, shaking, plummeting planet.

The Rescue. Second Officer Mark Thomas made an interesting comment about Captain Cronin's handling of the mid-air crisis on Flight 811. He attributed the salvation of 345 shaken people to a pilot's personal courage and experience, not to the textbook rules of flight. "They give you air speeds for two engines out. They give you air speeds for partial flaps," Thomas said. "But they don't give you air speeds for two engines out, partial flaps, and a huge hole in the side of the airplane."

The salvation of even one of us will not be a textbook affair either. Rules will not be sufficient to rescue us from sin, death, and hell. Judged by the rules, the verdict is clear: "There is no one righteous, not even one" (Rom. 3:10). "Therefore no one will be declared righteous in his sight by observing the law," wrote Paul, "rather, through the law we become conscious of sin" (Rom. 3:20). "For it is by grace you have been saved, through faith — and this not from yourselves, it is the gift of God — not by works, so that no one can boast" (Eph. 2:8-9).

Passengers on jets in trouble generally don't storm the cabin, take the controls in their own hands, and shove the pilot out of his chair. In the matter of salvation, however, that is precisely our tendency. Rather than accepting grace through faith, we try to work our way into God's favor through our own good deeds. Rather than trusting what Jesus did at the cross, we structure our own systems of righteousness. It is the height of spiritual folly.

Rather than trusting what Jesus did at the cross, we structure our own systems of righteousness.

All we need do is to trust the one who is at the controls. Listen to his instructions. Follow his orders. Obey him without indecision. But realize that you are not saving yourself in your repentance, your baptism, your prayers, your Christ-imitating deeds. Jesus is the pilot-savior, and we are simply passengers-disciples who are learning to trust him to get us through this white-knuckle trip. To present us spotless before the throne. To land us safely in heaven.

Our Experience. What happens in the process of salvation can be described under a variety of metaphors. Each is only a metaphor, however, and is not an explanation of a process more complex and divine than we can understand.

Imagine how many times by now those 345 people have told their stories with their own illustrations. Trying to communicate what happened to them. Trying to depict their adventure for others. Each story is different, for each is told from a first-person perspective. Each is also the same, though, for each lived through the single experience of being brought from what appeared to be certain death to safety.

The Bible speaks to the person who is enslaved by sex, drugs, or greed and represents the experience of salvation as "redemption." Jesus is the one who "gave himself for us to redeem us from all wickedness and to purify for himself a people that are his very own, eager to do what is good" (Tit. 2:14).

It speaks to the neglected, abused, and lonely person and depicts salvation as "adoption" into the family of God. "In love he predestined us to be adopted as his sons through Jesus Christ, in accordance with his pleasure and will" (Eph. 1:5).

It addresses the defeated and broken person who sees no way to resolve the chaos of her life and weeps for the chance to start over with a clean slate and describes salvation as being "born again." "But when the kindness and love of God our Savior appeared, he saved us, not because of righteous things we had done, but because of his mercy. He saved us through the washing of rebirth and renewal by the Holy Spirit, whom he poured out on us generously through Jesus Christ our Savior" (Tit. 3:4-6; cf. John 3:1ff).

I have been on only one flight which was so frightening that the passengers broke out in applause for our captain when he brought the ship down safely. I made it a point to go by the cabin door, to shake his hand, and to tell him how grateful I was. What must it have been like on Flight 811! Those people will never stop singing the praises of Captain David Cronin.

And that is the mission of the church in a nutshell: *to sing the praises of our Savior.* That is our reason for being. Our justification for existing. To let people know of the only hope any one of us has for life.

> "Man of Sorrows," what a name
> For the Son of God who came
> Ruined sinners to reclaim!
> Hallelulah! What a Savior!

Section Two

Hope

How to Revive
a Dream

Discovery roared into orbit on September 29, 1988, 32 months after the tragic *Challenger* explosion which took seven lives and shattered a nation's euphoric confidence in its space program. With the majestic rise of the space shuttle into its orbit 184 miles above Earth, America's dream of space exploration was reborn.

An engagement is called off. A business fails. A child dies. An accident leaves someone a quadraplegic. In each case, someone's dream dies.

If you are suffering the heartbreak of having something snatched away from you, don't give in to self-pity. Don't accept failure as your inevitable fate. If the dream was worth having in the first place, go back to the drawing board to refine it. Then launch a renewed, refined project aimed at a worthwhile goal.

Remember Moses' failed dream of rescuing his people? He acted on his own initiative and at a time of his own choice. It blew up in his face. Forty years later, God acted through him to redeem a nation of two million.

Remember the crushed dreams of two disciples on the Emmaeus Road? They talked aloud to a third man who had joined them about daring to dream that Jesus was the Messiah. "We had hoped that he was the one who was going to redeem Israel," they lamented. Then the stranger revealed himself. Jesus was alive, and so was the dream of his disciples.

Remember a young man named Mark who wanted to work as a missionary apprentice with Paul but who turned back? His dream shattered, he left and went home. But Barnabas believed in him and gave him a second chance. He became valuable as a Christian teacher and wrote one of the four Gospels that survives to this day. He became quite a missionary after all.

God still revives dreams. He still gives courage to tired and broken dreamers. He still makes dreams come true.

The relationship may be rescued, or he may provide someone who is better for you. A lost job or failed business may be the prelude to discovering the niche which is just right for you. Whatever disappointment or failure you have experienced need not be final. God is still able to work all things for good in the lives of his people.

The shuttle *Discovery* and its successful mission did not reverse the tragedy of *Challenger* or bring back seven astronauts. The tragedy of January 1986 remains forever. But the dream is still alive. And dreamers can unleash their creative energies again. Our manned space program need not remain mired in pain, disbelief, and uncertainty.

Whatever disappointment or failure you have experienced need not be final.

Your life need not be stalled forever by the broken dream you are grieving over today. Get back to the drawing board. Go there on your knees. Admit any fault in yourself that led to the failure, and restudy the basic design for your whole life. But don't stop dreaming.

The God who forgives sin and heals broken hearts can also turn dreams into reality.

Beauty Out of Chaos

When an artist begins a new canvas, he first puts down several broad strokes of basic colors. Someone watching him through an untrained eye might be confused and see no meaning at all to such a beginning. He might even walk away, convinced that nothing of beauty could come of so awkward a start.

As the artist works carefully to blend the colors and to introduce an occasional new one from his palette, however, what had originally seemed to be meaningless confusion begins to emerge into a beautiful painting.

The workings of our God are sometimes of the same order. He does this and allows that in his world. It might appear that in a given instance there is no possible good that can come from a situation. Then, as a skillful artist, he brings first this and then another influence to bear until something purposeful begins to emerge and some good work is done to his glory.

This is the biblical doctrine of *the providence of God.*

Divine providence should never be interpreted as meaning that every successful effort is a God-approved one or that every disaster is divine judgment. Wicked persons, such as Haman in the story of Esther, may prosper for a time and appear to be successful. At the same time, good persons may suffer as Satan attempts to undermine and destroy their faith in God. Witness the stories of Joseph and Job.

What had originally seemed to be meaningless confusion begins to emerge as a thing of beauty.

We are not infinite in wisdom and thus cannot see things as God sees them. We cannot always discern his reasons for allowing conditions which seem so unjust to us. We do know, however, that such unpleasant episodes as those which have been endured by Joseph, Esther, or many a modern-day saint have perfected faith and strengthened character.

God is working on the canvas of human history. We must not presume to know what he is attempting to achieve in particular cases. Neither are we wise enough to be critical of his methods. His workings in our lives are beyond our ability to discern, and we may not understand them until we look back from eternity.

Beauty from chaos. Victory from defeat. Life from death. God has a track record of doing it time and again. So don't despair that you cannot see his resolution to your present crisis. Just continue to walk by faith, not by sight.

Sometimes the Reward Comes Later

It is easy to be misled by life's twists and turns. It confuses us when good goes unnoticed and unrewarded, while evil appears to prosper. Life can be terribly unfair. Solomon put it this way: "There is something else meaningless that occurs on earth: righteous men who get what the wicked deserve, and wicked men who get what the righteous deserve" (Eccl. 8:14).

I thought of this text the other day as I read about a Nashvillian who had been awarded a special medal from the United States government. The recognition came more than 40 years after the event it commemorated.

Bill Colsher was drafted into the U.S. Army in 1943. On October 7, 1944, when he was only 18 years old, he was captured by German forces. He was put into a prison camp at Luneburg in the Black Forest and kept there for over a year with 3,000 other Americans. He was then moved to Neubrandenburg and interred with 255 of his compatriots.

During two years and four months as a prisoner of war, he suffered terrible treatment. They first thought he was Jewish because of his last name. There was hard labor on a diet of bread, which was 60 percent sawdust, and thick, syrupy coffee.

As the war was nearing its end, his German captors heard that the Russians were advancing toward his camp. So all the prisoners were awakened at midnight and forced to march six days and nights away from the camp. Most died. Only about 20 of the original 256 lived through the ordeal.

In August of 1988, Mr. Colsher received a special medal for World War II Prisoners of War which honored him for his courage during the more than two years he spent in two German camps. At age 63, this employee of the Nashville Metropolitan Library was finally honored for his bravery.

Scripture supports the commonsense belief that doing right should lead to vindication and reward.

The expectation of a reward for doing right could be interpreted as sheer selfishness. But Scripture seems to support the commonsense belief that doing right should lead to vindication and reward. It is a fundamental notion of justice to believe that.

Rewards don't always come to people who deserve them. Sometimes they come much later than they should.

In either case, it is conceivable that someone who did a noble but still unrewarded deed would wonder whether it had been appreciated. Whether it was worth doing in the first place. Whether he would do it again under the same or similar circumstances.

Paul endured hardships while dreaming of a crown of life which the Lord would give him at the end of time. Christians who were suffering under Roman persecution at the end of the first century had to be encouraged to faithfulness with the reminder that their reward might never come in this life.

You may need to remember the same thing today. Your reward for faithfulness to your mate, seeing your child through a tough time, or integrity at your job may not come today. Your return for serving behind the scenes or bearing reproach for Jesus' name may not come tomorrow. Or next month. Or in this lifetime.

That a Christian has done *the right thing* is not determined by how it is perceived today. Or by instant appreciation. Or by a quick reward. But by *faithfulness* to the Lord Jesus.

"I have fought the good fight, I have finished the race, I have kept the faith," wrote Paul. "Now there is in store for me the crown of righteousness, which the Lord, the righteous Judge, will award to me on that day, and not only to me, but also to all who have longed for his appearing" (2 Tim. 4:7-8).

The exalted Christ wrote to the church at Smyrna: "Be faithful, even to the point of death, and I will give you the crown of life" (Rev. 2:10b).

Bill Colsher waited over 40 years for his reward. You may have to wait until the Day of the Lord for yours.

Courage to Begin Again

John Callender was an officer under George Washington in the Revolutionary War. He failed miserably during the Battle of Bunker Hill and was dismissed from the army for behaving as a coward. On his papers, Gen. Washington wrote: "Cowardice, a crime of all others the most injurious, and the last to be forgiven."

To his credit, Callender allowed his shame and embarrassment to move him to try to make up for what he had done and to redeem his good name. So he re-enlisted in the army as a private and so conducted himself at the Battle of Long Island that Washington reinstated him as a captain and revoked his earlier sentence.

The true story of John Callender has a lesson in it for all of us. Nobody goes through life without episodes of weakness, failure, and humiliation. Those with the courage to begin again are people to be admired.

It isn't easy to be honest with yourself about sin. The human tendency is to be defensive and proud. But the religion of Jesus Christ teaches us that such a spirit hinders recovery. "God opposes the proud but gives grace to the humble. . . . Grieve, mourn, and wail. Change your laughter to mourning and your joy to gloom. Humble yourselves before the Lord, and he will lift you up" (James 4:6, 9-10).

Nobody goes through life without episodes of weakness, failure, and humiliation.

In spite of the difficulty in beginning again, there is even a way to learn from past failures and to achieve successes that might have been impossible otherwise. This time you know the things to avoid, the dangerous temptations that can turn you aside from your goal, and the weaknesses within yourself. Having failed and knowing what contributed to that failure, you can take steps to guarantee success in the new effort.

Nobody ever failed more miserably than Peter. He was a chosen apostle, special friend to the Lord, and leader among his peers. But he fled when Jesus was arrested (Matt. 26:56b) and denied him three times in the high priest's courtyard (Matt. 26:69-75). When Jesus later gave Peter a chance to begin again (John 21:15-23), he took it and made the best of it.

Look at your own situation today. If you are grieving over failure, sin, and confusion in your life, have the courage to throw yourself on the mercy of God for forgiveness and to begin again.

When the Wrong Thing Is the Right Thing

Foolish things can be wise. Disastrous things can be glorious. "Wrong" things can be right.

Susan Dzialowy is a good case study of the sort of thing I have in mind. She is a 27-year-old Chicagoan. She is married and the mother of three children, daughters eight and seven, a son five. Christmas 1988 was going to be rough for the Dzialowys because Susan's husband, John, was out of work. But they were doing the best they could.

On Christmas Eve, while John had gone for groceries, a space heater in the family's Southwest Side home caught their apartment on fire. Within a matter of minutes, flames were shooting through the windows. Thick smoke was everywhere. Susan bolted outside. She looked immediately to see if her three children had escaped, and they were nowhere in sight.

She turned back without hesitating and went inside the building to try to rescue them. I wish I could tell you that the story has a happy ending. It doesn't.

Susan was overcome by the heat and smoke. Fire-fighters arrived on the scene and found her unconscious in the rear bedroom. They attempted cardio-pulmonary resuscitation at the scene and transported her to St. Anthony's Hospital. She never regained consciousness.

What about her children? They were safe the whole time. They had escaped on their own when the fire started. So Susan's heroic act of motherly devotion was, on one view of things, unnecessary. Her death a foolish waste. Her decision wrong.

At the hospital, the children told their mother, "Mommy, get up. We want you to come home and have Christmas with us." Her husband kept shaking his head and saying that he and the children never even had the chance to tell Susan goodbye.

In a fairy tale, the story would have ended differently. Susan would have lived. In fact, she, her husband, and their three children would have "lived happily ever after." But reality is frequently very different from fairy tales.

Because Susan's story ends tragically, does that prove she did something foolish? That she shouldn't have gone back? That she was wrong to do so?

Americans, you see, are prone to judge the conduct of an event by its outcome. If a politician gets elected, he ran his campaign well. When a woman gets promoted to vice president of the company, she "must be doing something right." Should a businessman make a fortune, he's a huge success. On the other hand, the candidate who loses, the woman who gives up her career to be a mother, the businessman who goes bankrupt, or the would-be rescuer who dies in a futile and unnecessary mission is a schmuck. A numskull. A failure.

Hold on! The politician who gets elected or the woman who becomes company vice president by dirty tricks and unprincipled behavior is *not* a winner. The woman who trades a corporate office for a family, a man who goes bankrupt because he won't bribe a union or government official, and Susan Dzialowy are not life's dopes, nincompoops, and rejects. They give up career for children, risk profit for principle, and give up personal survival for the sake of imperiled offspring.

Vindication for doing right doesn't always come at the moment the deed is done.

By virtue of our American pragmatism, we either judge these people harshly or throw them a bone of condescending sympathy. From the standpoint of biblical witness, they are heroic figures.

Vindication for doing right doesn't always come at the moment the deed is done. In a society which stresses immediate outcomes and instant recognition, it is hard to keep one's perspective. Passing up personal safety or letting a chance for success go by would be considered idiotic by lots of people. Foolish. Wrong.

So a teen-ager has sex rather than be called a prude or does drugs rather than be dubbed a coward. A yuppie spends irresponsibly and lives immorally. A politician lies and sells influence. A misunderstood husband and a neglected wife have an affair. A preacher builds his own kingdom rather than God's. There seems to be no end to it.

In this world which has put evil for good and darkness for light, it takes a conscious effort to keep our thinking straight. We have to remind ourselves that doing what others may not be able to understand or approve, what they may even call ridiculous and wrong, is often right.

From the standpoint of what was in her best interest, Susan Dzialowy did a risky, foolish, and wrong-headed thing. From the point of view of her parental devotion, Susan did what was *right* for a mother or father to do in the situation. That the episode ended tragically does not change that.

Joseph did the right thing to refuse Potiphar's wife, even if he had rotted in jail. The kid who refuses to cheat on an exam does right, even if he makes the lowest grade in the class because everyone else did cheat. The salesman does right who tells the truth about his product's limitation, even if he misses the sale on account of it. The woman who is faithful to her husband and works through the problems in their marriage does right, even if she could have spared herself a lot of grief by leaving the jerk years ago.

Other people may think you are foolish. They may wag their heads and chide you for being naive. They may call what you do "unnecessary" or "idiotic" or "wrong." By *their* standards, maybe so. In the *short term*, perhaps.

Judged by the amount of *heartache* it purchases for you today, unquestionably.

Yet you have a long-term view in mind. You believe in a God who does not abandon his people who keep faith with him by doing what is right. A God who rewards faithfulness. If not in this life, then in the one to come.

Isn't the Christian faith predicated on an event which illustrates this truth? Jesus' perfect righteousness and willing obedience to the Father in heaven were not rewarded with applause. He was despised and rejected. He was betrayed and flogged. He was denied justice and condemned to die. Yet his weakness and foolishness were ultimately turned into power and wisdom. The same thing has been true of saints, apostles, and martyrs through the centuries.

Scripture has no Pollyanish view of life. No happily-ever-after theology of how right decisions are always vindicated just at the last moment and before any harm comes. Just the realistic and challenging call: "Be faithful, even to the point of death, and I will give you the crown of life" (Rev. 2:10).

Dare to Sing . . .
Others Will Join In

     I didn't get to watch much of the 1988 Olympic Games from Seoul. One or two dives by Greg Louganis. Less than five minutes of basketball. A couple of replays of running events. There is one event from those games, however, I regret not getting to see. In fact, I would have liked to have been in the arena when it happened.

     Taekwando is not even an Olympic event. It is one of three basic martial arts, with Chinese kung fu and Japanese karate. It was a demonstration sport in the 1988 games.

     America's welterweight representative in taekwondo competition was Arlene Limas. At the time of the games, she was a 22-year-old senior in pre-law at DePaul University. Although she was the U.S. national champion in 1987, she wasn't expected to "bring home the gold" from Seoul. But she won an upset victory in her division. So there she was. Standing on the high center riser for the awards ceremony. Wearing her gold medal around her neck. The American flag began to go up.

But the tape machine broke, and there was no music. The standing crowd in Changchung Gymnasium began looking around. Arlene was bewildered as to why the anthem wasn't playing. So she began singing *The Star-Spangled Banner.* Then someone joined her. Her parents. GIs in the stands. Other Americans who were there as spectators. Arlene Limas moved her arms up and down to lead the crowd in an *a cappella* performance of the national anthem. An athlete had become a conductor.

Someone with the courage to make the first move can channel the energy of a host of others.

It had to be the most moving awards ceremony of the 1988 Olympic Games. Tears were streaming down faces all around the arena. A formality had been transformed into a never-to-be-forgotten event. One girl's unsteady voice provided the overture for an impromptu chorus.

This sort of thing happens frequently in less-dramatic, less-public settings.

One teen-ager in the frightened group says no to the kid offering them drugs, and the rest get the courage to do the same thing.

A member of the board summons the heart to suggest that the company adopt a policy which puts principle above profit, and a chorus of seconds comes from around the conference table.

A white family goes to visit the first minority family to move into its neighborhood and invites them to dinner in their home that night, and the tension on that block vanishes as others decide to follow their example of acceptance.

God's people are called to be light and salt in this world. And sometimes to be singers. *Leadership* often comes without title or fanfare. The situation calls for action, and someone with the courage to make the first move can channel the energy of a host of others.

Maybe there's a situation just around the corner in your life which will call for you to be a leader. Don't panic. Yes, you're only one person. One six-billionth of Earth's masses. But if you will open your mouth and sing your song, it might surprise you how many other voices join in.

She Became
Good for Something

One of the vaguest concepts in the minds of most believers is "goodness." I have struggled to give the idea specific content in my mind. Perhaps one way to do it is by means of a contrast.

Do you know the expression "good for nothing"? Well, a Christian is *good for something*. He has purpose to life in glorifying God. She sees her mission each day in terms of sharing the knowledge of God. One who believes in the Lord Jesus Christ wants his life to count for all that is holy and right.

My friend had been an alcoholic for several years. It had been over three years since she had gone a full day without drinking heavily. To use her own words, she was a "typical, good-for-nothing drunk." She couldn't keep her house, love her husband, or be a mother to her children.

Then the goodness of God led her to repentance and recovery. Unlike some alcoholics who get jolted back to their senses by accident, illness, or family disintegration, she was brought back to hers by the fact that her husband and two girls wouldn't leave her or give up on her. They stayed, suffered with her, and prayed that she would find a way to deal with her problem.

To use her own words, she was a "typical, good-for-nothing drunk."

The undeserved, continued love of her family moved her to confess her sin. She committed herself to a strategy of coping with her disease by God's grace. Alcoholics Anonymous gave her a support group which really understood her situation. Christian friends stood with her, prayed for her, and encouraged her and her family. A sister in Christ who is a recovering alcoholic was her AA sponsor.

Change began to occur in her life. There were extremely difficult times for a while, with occasional setbacks and failures. But the power of God to transform was allowed to work in her life. She not only stopped drinking but also began to function again as a whole person within her world.

It has been several years now since she has touched alcohol. Her family life is idyllic. She teaches Sunday School. Nobody who has come to know her within the past three years would ever dream that she was once a "good-for-nothing drunk." Now she is a *good-for-something disciple* of the Lord Jesus!

And do you know what she is best at? You've probably guessed already. She counsels alcoholics and has helped a number of men and women find a way to get free of an awful addiction.

Such is the nature of Christian "goodness." It points one toward the goal of being useful for a specific purpose. Understood this way, each of us can examine himself for the presence of this Christian virtue in daily life.

The Language of Victory

People say, "Everybody loves a winner!" But our actions make me doubt it. Sometimes we appear to resent and to want to bring down the person who does something notable. Remember Yahweh's boast about Job: "Now there's a decent fellow"? But Satan slandered him: "Yeah. Who wouldn't be in his place? He has everything!"

We humans can be as cynical as the devil about other's successes. At the same time, we can be surprisingly helpful and compassionate toward the person on hard times. Perhaps it is easier to condescend than to congratulate, to weep with those who are weeping than to rejoice with those who are rejoicing.

Maybe worse still, however, is the inability of many people to live in victory themselves. It's as if those people have convinced themselves that they deserve to be losers. Failure is more acceptable than winning for them. They program their lives to fail.

You don't believe it happens? What of the girl in junior high who makes good grades or wins the science fair competition only to be made fun of or shut out by her classmates? Next time she deliberately does poorly on the exam or turns in a botched project lest she be a victim of her classmates' insecurities or envy again.

People can be programmed for failure in a variety of ways. Some are brainwashed as children to believe they are "ugly," "dumb," or "clumsy." Heard often enough from significant persons in their lives, these words become self-fulfilling prophecies.

A lot of people suffer from low self-esteem. They think they deserve to fail, so they constantly sabotage themselves. They fail in order to confirm their harsh judgments of themselves.

Others fear success lest people expect even more of them in future settings. Because they don't believe they can perform well consistently or improve so as to live up to the demands which might follow, they abort the process with a failure.

And some people have been positively taught that it is evil to enjoy success. "While you're playing on that new bike, Johnny," says his mother, "I hope you don't forget that many children in the world won't be getting any presents on their birthdays." Thus Johnny learns to feel guilty in connection with good fortune, and it goes with him through life.

I'm ready to reject the notion that failure is some-how more spiritual than success. Lately we've done a better job in helping people deal with crisis, pain, and failure by teaching more about grace. But we've done a poor job helping people cope with victory, joy, and success without feeling guilty over them.

Perhaps the key to the solution of this problem is found at 2 Corinthians 2:14: "But thanks be to God, who always leads us in triumphal procession in Christ and through us spreads everywhere the fragrance of the knowledge of him." Christians are winners! We march in the triumphal procession of our Lord!

We've done a poor job helping people cope with victory, joy, and success without feeling guilty over them.

The very language of that verse makes you want to stand erect and stick out your chest. It promotes the good feelings of personal worth and significance which all of us need. But here comes the irony which the worldly mind will never understand: *The language of triumph belongs only to those people who know they deserve nothing better than hell.*

A life of victory and triumph is lived with Jesus Christ. It does not relate so much to *what you do* as it does to *who you are.* You are Christ's. He has redeemed you, washed you in his blood. You are heaven-bound in him.

So, whether promoted or laid off, you are secure in him. Whether healthy or disabled, you have a purpose for your life. Whether driving a new car or an old clunker, you feel good about your identity as a child of the King. Regardless of your circumstances, you evaluate all things in spiritual perspective and know that you are a winner in Christ.

With Christ at the center of your new world-view, things are changed. Harsh self-judgments and low self-esteem can give way to a positive self-image of Christ. "Therefore, if anyone is in Christ, he is a new creation; the old has gone, the new has come! And this is from God, who reconciled us to himself through Jesus. . . " (2 Cor. 5:17).

Whatever is crippling you from the past in terms of the brainwashing you have undergone can be overcome. Instead of buying the old doubts and limitations, you can begin to believe in your new possibilities. "I can do everything through him who gives me strength," said Paul (Phil. 4:13). In the same epistle where these words are found, he had earlier talked about "forgetting what is behind and straining toward what is ahead" (cf. Phil. 3:12-14). It was Christ's strength that turned him around, that transformed defeatist thinking into the language of victory.

Learning to think with a Christian mind, it will finally dawn on you that there is no such thing as "losing" for God's faithful people. Does someone sacrifice for Christ's sake? Here are Jesus' words on sacrifice: "I tell you the truth, no one who has left home or brothers or sisters or mother or father or children or fields for me and the gospel will fail to receive a hundred times as much in this present age (homes, brothers, sisters, mothers, children and fields — and with them persecutions) and in the age to come, eternal life" (Mark 10:29-30). And what about death? Even that is victory for the people of God. Paul wrote: "For to me, to live is Christ and to die is gain" (Phil. 1:21).

It is high time for Christians to abandon the vocabulary of defeat. Nothing is going to happen to us in this life which cannot be dealt with in his strength. Even in events the world might see as tragedy, God's people see an opportunity for divine power to give victory. As I told Jackie during his final illness, "There's no way you can lose, brother. Either you'll recover to serve God with your restored health, or you'll go to be with the Lord sooner than you'd thought. Either way you win!"

Nothing is going to happen to us in this life which cannot be dealt with in his strength

---

Since Christ fought a battle which didn't really belong to him, we share in a triumph which isn't really ours. There's no pride on our part. No arrogant boasting. Just humble confidence. Our weak faith coupled with his mighty power makes us "more than conquerors through him who loved us" (Rom. 8:37).

Don't be afraid to achieve. Don't hide your gifts out of false modesty or fear that others might resent their use. Do whatever you do unto the Lord, knowing that he deserves your very best. Give him glory rather than taking it for yourself. And know that a victory consecrated to the Lord is holy. You don't have to program yourself to fail in order to be spiritual.

I've Had a Change
of Heart

Jimmy Moore was a dying man. There just wasn't any future for him. Then he got his chance at life again in the form of a heart transplant at Vanderbilt Hospital. Two years later, he completed the grueling Music City Triathlon which consists of a kilometer-long swim, 40-kilometer bike ride, and 10-kilometer run.

Jay Groves, coordinator of Vanderbilt's cardiac rehab program, ran and bicycled with Jimmy. Frieda Fowinkle came in from Atlanta to be with him during the swimming portion of the event.

The man who had a heart transplant 18 months earlier crossed the finish line with tears in his eyes and these words across the front of his T-shirt: "I've had a change of heart."

Paul likened his experience in living for Christ to running a race and receiving the crown of righteousness (2 Tim. 4:7-8). And the book of Hebrews exhorts believers to "run with perseverance the race marked out for us" (Heb. 12:1).

Like Jimmy Moore, anyone who finishes this race and receives a reward will have had a "change of heart."

A *cold heart* will have to be warmed by the love of God.

A *hard heart* will have to give way to a sensitive one.

A *rebellious heart* will be replaced by an obedient heart.

If it is true that one's heart is the "wellspring of life" (Prov. 4:23), it is no wonder that God has to operate on it. The reason a life ever gets out of control is heart disease. The wellspring of life gets polluted or diverted from its course. It erodes value and self-esteem, washes away the moorings of right living, and floods a person's life with destructive force.

Our hearts have to be given over to God, totally and without reservation.

More often than not, you and I don't understand our own hearts. We can't explain why we feel the way we feel or do some of the things we do. That is exactly the reason why our hearts have to be given over to God, totally and without reservation.

> The people who used to know foul-mouthed, hard-drinking Rob can't believe what they see in him now.
> Jill's parents are grateful to have back the daughter they knew before a two-year rebellion put her on the streets.
> Helen and Vick's marriage was chaotic until they both got serious about doing God's will a few months ago.

People like these might well stride through the pearly gates wearing T-shirts saying "I've had a change of heart." And, to use the words of Jimmy Moore about his run, each of them would say to you: "If I can do it, anybody can do it."

Making Your Curse Your Calling

Bad things happen to all of us. Some people seem to get more than their share, but nobody is exempt.

You haven't been singled out. You're not the first to have something terrible happen to you. And getting through this ordeal isn't like having measles. It will not grant you immunity from the next outbreak.

The important thing, then, is not some secret path for escaping misfortune but a strategy which will enable you to cope with it. And one of the best case studies I've come across recently is the story of Marie Balter.

In November of 1988, Marie began work as an administrator at Danvers State Hospital in Boston. It is a mental hospital. More significantly still, it is the same mental hospital where she spent 17 years as a patient. Here is the broad outline of her story . . .

At age 17, Marie Balter went through some very difficult personal ordeals and became clinically depressed.

She was misdiagnosed, labeled schizophrenic, and sent to Danvers. She stayed there for the next 17 years of her life!

After persistent friends worked to get her out, she was finally released from the hospital in 1964. She went back to school and wrote an autobiography which was the basis of a 1986 made-for-TV movie, *Nobody's Child*, which starred Marlo Thomas.

She lectured across the nation. She worked with psychiatric patients. She earned a masters degree from Harvard. Now she is at work as community affairs director at the hospital which was once her prison.

You can use your past experiences to reach out to others who are suffering through things you once lived.

Here is a lady who made what had been her curse into her calling. Her personal bane into a blessing for others. A world of pain and horrible memories into a ministry.

What is her rationale for passing over the bitterness most of us would be tempted to wallow in after such an experience? "I don't believe in focusing on all the bad stuff," she says. "Everybody has problems. Life is not trouble free."

And what of her attitude toward the people responsible for what happened to her? "Forgiving is a way of reaching out from a bad past and heading out to a more positive future," asserts the 58-year-old Balter. "I wouldn't have grown if I didn't learn to forgive."

You've suffered injustices, haven't you? Had some awful things happen to you because of someone else's foul-up? Had to fight the urge to strike back?

Try to put yourself in Marie Balter's shoes. Imagine her getting out of the hospital, seething with rage, and striking out against the institution and people who had done that horrible thing to her. What ultimate good do you think would have come from it? Then contrast that with what she is doing with her life now. Setting aside personal revenge, she is changing things that will make a difference in the lives of other people.

What is your prison today? Perhaps it is grief. The loss of a job. Scars from sexual abuse you suffered as a child. Unfair treatment at your job. Cancer. Depression. Divorce. Slights from Christians who should know better.

There is an alternative to bitterness, vindictiveness, and retaliation. Realizing that life isn't fair to any of us, refuse to focus on the bad things. Forgive some people, and turn loose some grudges. Ask God to purge your heart of resentment and let you go on with your life.

Better still, use your past experiences of pain to reach out to others who are suffering through things you understand from your own background. Turn something that has been your misfortune into someone else's blessing by letting God make you a minister of his grace.

It's a far better approach than carrying it around for the rest of your life as a burden of bitterness.

Perspective

Most of us have difficulty at times keeping things in perspective. So we magnify obstacles. Overemphasize our importance to projects. Think too critically about ourselves after a time of failure or too highly of ourselves after an achievement.

Ever heard (or *said*) anything similar to these tried-and-true paradigms of lost perspective?

"I'll just die if he doesn't ask me to be his date to Homecoming / if this promotion doesn't come through / if I'm not married by the time I'm 30."

"I'll never get over it if he leaves me / if she dies / if we can't have a baby."

"I'd rather be dead than be humiliated because the affair has been exposed / because my son has AIDS / because of going into treatment for drug addiction."

At the 1988 winter Olympics, Dan Jansen was given a good chance to win gold medals in speed-skating. In his best event, the 500-meters, he crashed and fell coming out of the first turn. Later, in the 1,000-meters, skating at a gold-medal pace and two-thirds through the event, he caught a skate blade in the ice on a straightaway and tumbled in a heap.

Nobody has to be destroyed by mistakes, sins, or personal tragedy. We can even learn and grow from them.

Years of discipline, training, and hoping went sprawling on the ice with him. He must have been devastated. But he handled it with such grace. "What happened in the last week has absolutely put things in a different perspective," Jansen said, "and I don't feel as bad as I would have."

You see, his 27-year-old sister had died earlier on the day of his first race. It put his failure to win an Olympic medal in perspective for him.

Whatever you've done is probably neither as wonderful nor as dreadful as you are tempted to think it is. Someone else can do better. Many others have done worse. God is still on his throne, and life goes on.

Nobody has to be destroyed by his mistakes, sins, or personal tragedies. Some even learn from them. They experience personal growth. They teach the rest of us to keep things in clearer focus. They find God.

Good at What You Hate

Ed Greer was on the fast track at Hughes Aircraft in El Segundo, California. He was an aerospace executive, struggling up the corporate ladder in a world of white collars and pinstripes. But he hated his work. He felt trapped.

One day he told a co-worker: "Never become too good at something you hate. They'll make you do it the rest of your life."

On September 10, 1981, Ed Greer disappeared. There was a police report. His father-in-law offered $100,000 for information about his whereabouts.

The impression spread among the people who had worked with him that there hadn't been foul play. They were of the opinion that he had dropped out on life in the pressure cooker. Resigned the rat race. Taken up the vagabond life he had dreamed about.

As a matter of fact, his former colleages envied him while they stayed at their work. They began throwing annual parties. Some of them would wear Ed Greer masks. They said they wished they had the courage to do what he had done.

The FBI found him in Houston seven years after he disappeared, and his story became public knowledge via a *Los Angeles Times* story in February of 1989.

Living under the name Roy Hearn, he was working for an oil exploration firm. But he had spent a lot of those seven years as a vagabond beach bum. He would occasionally fix a boat engine to make some money. Then he would lounge on the beach. "There are a lot of pretty girls on the beach," he explained.

People can get trapped. They can get painted into corners. Become resentful. Seethe with anger. Eventually, perhaps, do something irresponsible. Most, though, keep on plodding. Getting ulcers. Having migraines. Snapping at the kids. Grumbling at everything going on in the church.

Maybe Ed Greer was giving good advice when he said you should never become "too good at something you hate" lest somebody should force you to keep doing it the rest of your life.

A young person shouldn't become a doctor just because she's good at math or get an M.B.A. because there is a family business he is supposed to keep going into the fourth generation. The fact that you have a certain skill or ready-made position doesn't necessarily mean you should commit to it. Is there fulfillment in it for you? Is it something you want to do? Or do you hate it? It is better to be honest from the start and do something worthwhile with your life than to live someone else's expectation.

Someone occasionally makes a choice to do something he really likes, works at it a while with a sense of fulfillment, but comes to a point that he wants to make a career change. But it's risky. Someone warns him about the sacrifice of scaling down lifestyle and starting over. And there is a car payment, boat payment, and mortgage. So he's trapped and resentful. He may not pull an Ed Greer stunt. But he may opt for something almost equally bizarre. Perhaps an affair or experimentation with cocaine.

It is better to be honest from the start and do something worthwhile with your life than to live someone else's expectation.

Whole families sometimes get in predicaments of habit and expectation. He shreds his wife's ego with verbal switchblades because he is good at quick wit and sarcasm, but he hates himself later for the humiliation he knows he caused her before their friends. She is good at manipulating him with tears or sex or pouting, but she hates herself for getting her way by exploiting him. And children can become accomplished at duping and misleading their naively trusting parents, yet they may feel rotten and hate themselves for taking advantage of love.

Then there are people who are "too good at something they hate" in the form of addictive behaviors. Some women are too good at cooking and hate their compulsive eating and weight gain. Some men and women are too good at charming and flirting and cheating, though they genuinely hate it when they occasionally face up to what their moral principles demand and what they are doing to people they love. Some are so good at the party life and drinking, but they hate it that they increasingly can't stop before blacking out or causing problems. They've become too good at something they hate.

You don't have to do something you hate for the rest of your life. You don't have to live as a trapped and caged tiger. You don't have to stifle resentment and be what someone else has decided you must be, make yourself the extension of someone else's frustrated ambition, or stay hooked to a self-destructive behavior. But the answer isn't to become an Ed Greer and just vanish into irresponsible oblivion.

You can be honest. You can explore other options for your life. You can make some sacrifices to get ready for and undertake a career change in a responsible manner. You can find resources which will help you break out of patterns of behavior which are killing you but which have enslaved you.

Jesus valued, talked about, and offered *freedom*. Freedom from the slavery of sin. Freedom from the ruts and traditions of a stuffy heritage. Freedom from the monotony of a life which means nothing and drifts aimlessly.

So remember the good advice of a fellow who got trapped only to break out of his prison irresponsibly. And, if you're in the same boat, admit it and begin exploring some new options. With the courage to take charge of your own life under God, seek his grace to act wisely and to live abundantly.

"Never become too good at something you hate. They'll make you do it the rest of your life."

Pie in the Sky
vs. Main Course

Near the close of the book of Revelation, John was allowed a glimpse of heaven. He saw a crystal-clear river flowing from the throne. He saw the Tree of Life and realized that it was a perfect place, a place like Earth could never be. Then he heard this explanation:

> And I heard a loud voice from the throne saying, "Now the dwelling of God is with men, and he will live with them. They will be his people, and God himself will be with them and be their God. He will wipe every tear from their eyes. There will be no more death or mourning or crying or pain, for the old order of things has passed away."
>
> He who was seated on the throne said, "I am making everything new!" (Rev. 21:3-5a).

Karl Marx chided the notion of heaven as a distraction. A fantasy people can use to ease their pain rather than take up arms to change the world. A daydream which undermines serious involvement with the world. As a thoroughgoing materialist, he pleaded for people to reject what some call "pie in the sky by-and-by" in favor of commitment to the here-and-now world of the five senses.

Marx was wrong. Believing in heaven (and hell) does not diminish the importance of life on Earth; it magnifies its significance. Such a faith is not a coward's way of coping with unpleasant realities; it is the basis for courage in tackling them. It is not a means to escaping responsibility to the world; it is the justification for shouldering one's duties in the world. Let me explain.

If there is a heaven, my life has meaning. Eternal meaning.

If everything ends at the cemetery, there is no ultimate meaning to anything I do. I have no responsibility to anyone but myself. Trying to change the world would be the height of arrogance, for there would be no way of knowing that my vision of a better world was any better than that of my arch-enemy.

If there is a heaven, however, my life does have meaning. Eternal meaning. My freedom to make decisions is meaningful, for permanent consequences follow from those decisions. Morality is real. Love will conquer hatred, and good will triumph over evil.

So there is justification for facing and dealing with tough times. Caring about others. Telling the truth. Being involved with this world to try to improve it. Guide it toward God. Make it aware of its intended destiny.

The marvelous thing about heaven is that it is the Guiding Star of hope to the human soul. Paul put it this way: "Hope that is seen is no hope at all. Who hopes for what he already has? But if we hope for what we do not yet have, we wait for it patiently" (Rom. 8:24b-25).

I have a share in the Kingdom of God today. But the fullness of that kingdom has not yet come. There is frustration sometimes in waiting, but there is also excitement and anticipation. For the sake of everyone around me, I want to introduce whatever I can of the knowledge of Christ into my world. But if the world rejects both him and me, I recall that this world does not have the final say. This world is passing away, and when it is gone I will know Christ better in heaven than I can possibly know him here.

From the perspective of heaven, today's struggles and pains will only add zest to the triumph. Maternity wings in hospitals, after all, are not gloomy places. There is pain in giving birth. Tears. Even screaming. But those things are put into perspective when a mother holds her newborn baby.

> We know that the whole creation has been groaning as in the pains of childbirth, right up to the present time. Not only so, but we ourselves, who have the firstfruits of the Spirit, groan inwardly as we wait eagerly for our adoption as sons, the

redemption of our bodies. For in this hope we are saved (Rom. 8:22-24a).

The kingdom will come in its fullness when Jesus returns. The attendants waiting through the night will rejoice when the Bridegroom appears. The pains of labor will give way to the euphoria of birth. The farmer's patience will be justified by the harvest. "I consider that our present sufferings are not worth comparing to the glory that will be revealed in us" (Rom. 8:18).

Far from being pie in the sky, heaven is in the center of the believer's plate. Not dessert, but part of the main course. For faith cannot live without hope.

Section Three

Love

One Last Message

Jason Tuskes was a 17-year-old honor student in high school. He was very close to his mother, wheelchair-bound father, and younger brother. He was an expert swimmer. And he loved to scuba dive.

His final dive was in west-central Florida, not far from his home. He left home on a Tuesday morning to explore a spring and underwater cave. His plan was to be home in time to celebrate his mother's birthday by going out to dinner with his family that night.

Jason became lost in the cave. Then, in his panic, he apparently got wedged into a narrow passageway. He ran out of air and drowned.

When Jason realized he was trapped and doomed, he shed his yellow metal air tank and unsheathed his diver's knife. With the tank as tablet and the knife as pen, he wrote one last message to his family. Etched on the tank were these words: "I love you Mom, Dad and Christian."

Over the centuries, "God spoke to our forefathers through the prophets at many times and in various ways" (Heb. 1:1). They seldom listened. Even when they did hear God, they often defied him.

"In these last days he has spoken to us by his Son" (Heb.1:2). And how do we treat the Son of God? We seldom listen. When we do, we frequently choose to defy him. So the Sermon on the Mount goes unheeded. The messages from his parables fly past us. The things we hear in spite of ourselves more often simply aggravate us rather than change us.

God's final words to us are etched on a Roman cross. They scream to be heard.

But his final message. His dying communication. The meaning of his last few hours, minutes, seconds. Surely we can't be detached and indifferent. We must pay attention to the last communication to come from the final messenger of God to the human race.

God's final words to us are etched on a Roman cross. They are blood red. They scream to be heard.

The words are not the formal ones of a last will and testament. They are not the outraged ones of an innocent victim. They are not the anathemas of an angry judge. They are the generous, affectionate, merciful words of divine self-disclosure and hope.

Do you hear the words? From the cross, these words of God ring through the corridors of eternity: *"I love you."*

The Language God Speaks

Recently I was rereading the account of Paul's conversion found in Acts 26. It is the third telling of the story in Acts and is in Paul's own words as told before King Agrippa.

Something struck me from this reading that I had missed in all the times I have read it before: "We all fell to the ground, and I heard a voice saying to me *in Aramaic*, `Saul Saul, why do you persecute me?' "

Aramaic became the common tongue of the Jewish people as a result of the Babylonian captivity. For some reason, it seemed significant for Paul to point out that God spoke to him in his own language. As a matter of fact, it seems like a very important observation to make about our God that he comes to us just as we are.

Isn't that the meaning of the Incarnation? God became one with the human race he desired to save. Since we could not bring ourselves to his level, he came to ours.

Since we could neither think nor live heavenly lives, he humbled himself to live an earthly life with us.

Today God still speaks to us in language we can understand. He speaks to us in events of awe, such as the birth of a child. He speaks in the beauty of majestic mountains and brilliant flowers. He also speaks the language of comfort in our pain and deliverance in our bondage.

God speaks the language of joy. So he speaks in your prosperity as well as in your pain. He blesses you and is the source of every good gift.

It seems like a very important observation to make about our God that he comes to us just as we are.

Above all other ways, he speaks the language of love. In a church's fellowship, through your family, or by means of a genuinely caring friend, he speaks the language which reflects the essence of his nature.

It impressed Paul that God would speak his language. It also taught him how to relate to people. So to slave, free, Jew, Gentile, weak, or whomever he went with the message of Christ, Paul tried to speak their language. "I have become all things to all men so that by all possible means I might save some. I do all this for the sake of the gospel, that I may share in its blessings" (1 Cor. 9:22-23).

When we learn the same lesson, we will be more like God and more effective in sharing the gospel with the world.

Why Should We Love God?

Anyone who knows anything about Scripture can recite this verse: "Love the Lord your God with all your heart and with all your soul and with all your mind" (Matt. 22:37). According to Jesus, this is the first and greatest commandment of true religion.

But have you ever asked *why* you should love God? There is a lot of fuzziness in the minds of people on that one. And there is also a lot of prostitution of religion on account of the wrong-headed notions people give for why they love God.

To listen to the things some of us say, it appears that God is sometimes offered as a means to an end. Assuming we mean what we say, some people seem to love God in order to manipulate him to their purposes. We sneer at the big-screen gigolo who says "I love you" to woman after woman in order to use them. Why is it any holier for us to profess love for God in order to use him?

"I promised God that I would build a shelter for homeless children if he made my investment successful," says the financial wizard as he breaks ground for the building.

"Let my baby live! Spare his life, Oh God!" sobs a mother in the hospital waiting room. "I'll never be careless about spiritual things again and will raise him right."

"God, I hate this drinking and what it's done to my life," he prays. "Help me to put this stuff away for good, and I'll love you and serve you 'til I die!"

I suspect we've all bargained with God at one time or another. But when you see it written on paper, it looks shoddy and cheap, doesn't it? It is offering our love to God beneath a transparent veil of selfish reasons. In well-heeled, middle-class America, God must get a lot of this sort of devotion.

With the exiles from Judah captive in Babylon, Yahweh sent this word to them through the prophet Jeremiah: "You will seek me and find me when you seek me with all your heart" (Jer. 29:13).

And that is how we will find God! We must come without hidden agendas. No haggling over the price for our devotion. No tawdry contingent pledges of what we'll do only if he acts first.

We should love God simply because he is God. Not for what he might *do* for us, but for *who he is*.

Humankind has always wanted treasure, fame, comfort, release from struggle. Our latest effort is to have them in exchange for loving God, accepting Christ, or serving in the kingdom. Surely the love he wants is the same sort you and I desire: love for his very person rather than love for what he has that you might get.

But has he no concern for us? Is he unwilling to use his power for our sakes? Will he not answer those who call upon him in their times of need? Indeed, he will. For it is his nature to love his creatures and to give to them generously.

We must come without hidden agendas. No tawdry contingent pledges of what we'll do only if he acts first.

He wants us to ask in the assurance of receiving, to knock with the assurance that he will open, to seek knowing that he will be found. But all this he desires from trusting hearts who seek him and his righteousness for his own sake. Then all the blessings which come to you in due course or in response to specific requests you make can be received with delight and thanksgiving.

Here is the biblical statement of the principle at stake here: "But seek first his kingdom and his righteousness, and all these things will be given to you as well" (Matt. 6:33).

Recently I heard a man tell about going to the hospital after a call that his eight-year-old son had suffered a terrible fall from his bicycle and had hit his head on a concrete sidewalk. When he arrived, the doctor explained to him and his wife that the boy was in a coma and might not live.

The man told how he went into a phone booth, closed the door, and prayed. He didn't bargain. He didn't make any deals with God. He just prayed, "Lord, I love you, and I love my little boy. I put him in your hands and plead for your mercy. I ask that your will be done. Please let him live and be whole. If he is to die, let my wife and me have enough faith to praise you for eight years you let us have with him. In Jesus' name, Amen."

When God himself is the center around whom all your life revolves, either prosperity or adversity can be accepted and handled. If prosperity without pain is the goal and God the means to that, adversity means the collapse of faith and the abandonment of an unreliable instrument.

You can love him for his own sake. Or you can love him for the sake of using him, if that is love at all. The former is the means to secure faith; the latter contains the germ of its own destruction.

Why do *you* love God?

Kissing Ugly Girls

Harold Conrad, a former boxing writer who came to be known as a playwright and author, was talking about an experience with Muhammad Ali. "He's one of the kindest men I've ever known," he said. "A few years ago he took me to two prisons on a Sunday to visit convicts. I said, `Why are you doing this, Champ?' "

Ali answered, "All them people forgotten, somebody's gotta worry about 'em."

"One of the prisons was for women," continued Conrad. "All the inmates lined up and they were ooh-ing and aah-ing as he went along. And there were some good-looking ones. But he kissed only the ugly ones."

Later Conrad asked him to explain why, if he chose to kiss any of those women, he had picked only the ugly ones. "No one ever kisses 'em," responded the fighter who calls himself The Greatest, "and now they can remember that Ali kissed 'em."

Maybe you hear his statement as just another evidence of his own enlarged ego. It certainly seems to have none-too-subtle elements of egotism in it. But I think there is something else there as well.

It contains an acknowledgment by one human being of the need all others of us feel for positive stroking. Perhaps it even contains a barely-below-the-surface memory of times and places which were painful slights to a black man before he became wealthy and famous, the object of so much attention.

As I read it, this story isn't really about kissing at all. Or physical charms. It is about communication. Feelings. Security. And love. Mostly about love.

We speak of "benign neglect" in human relationships. But even if the oversight has no sinister intent, it can still hurt. Then, of course, there are those wicked attempts to hurt and humiliate another person through rudeness, coldness, and rejection.

People with no particularly distinguishing gifts or attributes get more than their share of exclusion. That, in turn, communicates to them their lack of desirability and reinforces their sense of isolation. Some get angry and do foolish or immoral things just to be noticed. Ever watch a two-year-old react to his newborn sister being the focus of attention or a "juvenile delinquent" in a classroom? Others simply accept that they are worthless and live out their self-perception.

Pretty girls get kissed. Straight-A students get complimented. Good athletes get cheered. Wealthy people get perks. High achievers get plaques.

Ugly girls seldom get kissed. Marginal students usually get chewed out by teachers and grounded by parents. Non-athletes don't hear many cheers. Poor people usually get yanked around. Folks with average skills doing average jobs just blend in with the woodwork.

Everybody needs affirmations of his or her intrinsic worth as a human being, a person in God's image. Performance (or lack of it) aside, people need to be noticed. Patted on the back. Hugged. Just because they are people.

Everybody needs affirmations of his or her intrinsic worth as a human being, a person in God's image.

A handshake is a more personal greeting than a nod or wave of the hand. Touching another human being deliberately closes the gaps, physical and emotional, between you and the other person.

A hug or kiss doesn't have to be a sexual overture. It can be (and in cultures such as the Russian, Greek, or French typically is) a warm greeting and a sign of friendship.

Even between married persons, their relationship needs to have casual, non-sexual touches. Pinkies linked. Hair touched. Arm-in-arm strolls.

Children who don't get enough holding as infants suffer for it in their physical and emotional health. Little ones need to sit on laps, ride on shoulders, and be hugged.

Then, even though most adolescents will affirm their independence by asking mom not to kiss them in the hall at church, they will be more secure and confident as they get through their turbulent and confusing teen years.

Words are good. But nothing is as straightforward and clear as a touch. As one writer put it: "Hugging, cuddling, snuggling, stroking, holding hands — the way we touch someone we care about is our most basic means of communication. It is one warm-blooded creature's saying to another, 'You're not alone. I'm here.' "

Ever wonder why Jesus "took the little children in his arms" to bless them? Touched the eyes of the blind man he healed? Even touched lepers?

Touching soothes our pain and makes us feel safe. It communicates that it is all right for us to be there. To feel what we are feeling. To put it into words. To share it with someone else.

Why not reach out and touch someone today? More specifically, try to reach out and touch someone who looks vulnerable, frightened, or hurt. Kiss a frog, and make him into a prince. Touch a forgotten soul, and make him into a king. Reach out to the children and the blind and the lepers, and be an instrument of your King.

Sharks and Dolphins

Dolphins are small mammals, varieties of which are found in all the oceans of the world. They communicate with one another by means of whistles, barks, and clicking sounds. They are among the most intelligent of animals and can be trained to do a variety of things.

If you have ever been to an aquarium, you may have watched them leap high into the air to take fish from a keeper's hand, jump through hoops, or play ball. Sailors and passengers on ships often see large schools of dolphins frolicking around their vessels. For centuries, seafaring men have held their appearance around their ships as an omen of smooth sailing.

Sharks are sea animals of another variety. Largest members of the fish family, sharks are insatiable eaters and fierce killers. With their several rows of long, sharp teeth, they gash and tear and kill.

Marine biologists explain that sharks appear to experience continual hunger. As one encyclopedia article puts it: "Their stomachs will not let them rest. Almost as soon as they eat they must be off after more food." Far from being a sign of anything festive, their appearance frightens people and empties beaches.

Adam McGuire was surfing about 300 feet off Half Tide Beach in Australia. The 17-year-old boy and two of his friends were unaware of the danger approaching them. A large shark went for him, gouged a chunk out of his surfboard, and knocked him into the water. Adam suffered a badly gashed abdomen from the initial attack.

Some people tear and slash their way through life. Others have a healing presence.

Then, just as suddenly as the shark had appeared, so did a school of dolphins. They swam for the shark. Got its attention. Distracted it from the injured boy. Alternately drew and chased it toward open water. In the meanwhile, Adam swam to shore. Police investigators credited the dolphins with saving Adam McGuire's life.

This incident, reported in American newspapers during the first week of 1989, reminded me that people also come in shark and dolphin varieties. Some folks tear and slash their way through life. They leave blood in their wake. They cause harm. Others have a healing presence. They make peace where there has been turmoil. They rescue strugglers who are going down for the third time.

Shark-types tend to talk loudly and make unreasonable demands; dolphin-types are under control and restrained in their expectations.

Some people threaten other people; others are secure enough in themselves that they don't need to throw their weight around.

Some have gluttonous appetites for money, sex, power, and attention; others have learned the power of self-control by the power of God's indwelling Spirit.

Some people can use, hurt, and throw away other people; others care about the welfare and feelings of the people in their world.

Some can destroy others, so long as they get what they want; others put themselves at risk or suffer loss rather than hurt someone else.

Some get even; others forgive.

Some live by hatred and taking; others live by love and generosity.

Sometimes I wish I could swim only in safe waters. Where there are no sharks. Where only playful dolphins brush close by and make me smile. Where there would be no threats, no harm, no panic. But that's not realistic, is it?

So, without being overly cynical, we'll all have to be on our guard in the ocean of life. Keeping watch against harm sneaking up on us. Looking around with caution always and skepticism occasionally. But somehow we must avoid becoming cynics. Pessimists about people. Frightened. Paranoid.

Finally, though you cannot choose temperaments and personalities for others, you *can* choose for yourself to be as you wish others were, to do unto others as you would have them do unto you.

And there will be one less predator in life's shark-infested waters.

When NOT to Help Someone

The general rule is that *decent people respond to others' pleas for help.* But there are exceptions to the rule. Sometimes loving people have to refuse to do things others have asked of them. Otherwise they wind up hurting the people they intended to be helping.

Is the general principle hard to accept? Does it sound unchristian to talk about turning down people who want your help? Maybe a case study will help get at the issue.

Joyce was a nurse whose alcoholism was killing her. Her supervisor had covered for her late arrival more than a few times, had sent her home "sick" on days when she came to work drunk, and had tried unsuccessfully to get her to enter a treatment program at her hospital. When Joyce came to work smelling of alcohol last week, she was fired.

Parents who want their children to get an education don't do their algebra homework for them or write their reports and term papers.

You don't do your friend a favor by lying to cover her absence from work, his cheating on his wife, or his addiction to cocaine.

The Bible tells church leaders to help the poor and feed the hungry, but it qualifies that obligation. Someone who is able to work but too lazy to do so should be allowed to go hungry. "For even when we were with you, we gave you this rule: 'If a man will not work, he shall not eat' " (2 Thess 3:10).

It is a misguided form of help which lets someone evade the responsibility he ought to be shouldering.

What's going on here? Are the principles of Christian ethics about helping others self-contradictory and inconsistent? Hardly! They are designed for our good.

It is a misguided form of help which lets someone evade the responsibility he ought to be shouldering.

Joyce tried laying a heavy guilt trip on her Christian supervisor. It didn't work, for the supervisor understood that Joyce would never face her need for help until somebody held her responsible for her behavior. The firing stands.

Students need to study. Adults must keep their commitments. It is only right for people creating problems to feel their pinch. Nobody should be encouraged to think that his life is a free ride which others subsidize.

Is the point coming clear now? You do not help someone by reinforcing a weakness. You are not loving and kind when you enable someone's flight from responsibility. Helping someone face up to and cope with a problem is one thing, but letting him deny and avoid it is something else again.

So if you are trying to help someone today, do your best to be sure you are really helping rather than hindering.

How to Create
"Hell on Earth"

I'm one of those old-fogey, conservative people who still believes the Bible. Believes that Jesus was raised bodily from the dead. That the world is moving to Judgment. That there is a real heaven and a real hell.

But some people seem not to be able to wait. They appear determined to experience a sample of hell right here on Earth.

In his *The Great Divorce*, C. S. Lewis pictures hell as an ever-expanding city with a progressive number of empty streets. He even describes the process of how it happens.

The people arriving in Lewis' hell are so quarrelsome that they pick fights with their neighbors within 24 hours of getting there. The run-ins are deemed unpleasant enough that within a week the newcomer decides to move. The next street over is usually empty, for everyone there has quarreled. If he moves to an inhabited street, the freshman is sure to have another argument soon and to move on.

The process continues. People get farther and farther apart. Before long they are thousands of miles from the bus stop where all the newcomers from Earth first arrive. Only by peering into a telescope can the latest arrivals see the lights of the occupied houses of grizzled old-timers who live millions of miles away, not only from the bus stop now but from each other as well.

Some research published recently says that a lack of social relationships in and of itself heightens peoples' susceptibility to illness and death. A University of Michigan study of 2,754 men and women in the United States, Finland, and Sweden says that *social isolation* "is as significant to mortality rates as smoking, high blood pressure, high cholesterol, obesity and lack of physical exercise."

The sort of isolation the study focused on is characterized by having nobody with whom you can share your private feelings, your innermost self. Estimates are that 10 to 20 percent of people have close contact with others less than once a week. They have acquaintances. Work in crowded buildings. Sit in packed church buildings. But their relationships don't have much quality to them. No depth. No satisfying warmth.

Social isolation is a growing trend. People are less likely to be married, to have a roommate, to involve themselves with people from their church, or to visit with friends. Strangely enough, the research shows that men are more devastated by isolation than women. The researchers say this is probably because women have a higher quality of relationships than men.

Not everybody who is isolated from people is that way from being disagreeable. Some people see themselves as unattractive, socially inept, or otherwise undesirable. Others fear they will be used, put down, or abandoned if they open up to someone else. And some have a self-image that tags them "unimportant" and "unlovable." We humans can be very harsh with ourselves.

People who feel their isolation from other human beings may blame the world for its coldness and unfriendly makeup. In which case they further isolate themselves by blaming and finger-pointing instead of doing something positive to end their loneliness.

Research shows that social isolation contributes as much to mortality rates as smoking, high blood pressure, and obesity.

Nobody can bring the detached 10 to 20 percent of a church, office, or world out of isolation and into the security of acceptance and love. The quarrelsome person has to lighten up. The frightened-of-closeness person has to push himself to open up once he gets to know and trust someone. The person who sees herself as unattractive or unlovable must try to find someone who will listen and give a candid reaction to the areas where she feels inadequate.

And that guilt-laden person who has isolated himself because he feels so ashamed, so unworthy, and so wretched must come to terms with whatever is locked away in the darkest corners of his or her heart. It must be laid open in the light of truth before God. It must be confessed to someone who is close enough to God's own heart that he will react with compassion rather than anathemas. It must be covered and washed away by the blood of Christ.

You've tried to come out of hiding and into the light? Someone betrayed you when you opened your heart to him? Hurt you and drove you farther underground? You just must summon up the courage to reach out again. And again and again, if necessary.

Do you fear that someone might reach out to you? Choose you to trust? Open the dark recesses of a closed, frightened, or guilty heart to you? You don't have to be scholarly. Say something profound. Know how to fix what is hurting that alienated soul. There are professional resources to draw on if the problem is severe. For most instances, however, you just need to listen. Weep with those who weep. Share what you know about the joy and peace of forgiveness in Christ. Just be there. Be "God with skin on" to hear, care about, and accept a lonely person into your heart and life.

There is already enough hell on Earth. Quarrelsome men. Defensive women. Frightened, lonely, and guilt-consumed people. People living in spiritual isolation from everyone else. If enough of us close gaps, reach out and touch one another, enter fellowship with each other, and love one another, who knows? In our families. In our churches. In our world. We just might create a little bit of *heaven* on Earth.

It's worth the risk of trying.

There Is a Difference
in the Touch

I am not a devotee of TV's soap operas. The story lines are generally shallow and predictable, and the acting tends to be incredibly poor. But an insight into Christ came the other day as I watched about three minutes of a "daytime drama."

The scene I watched had a physician examining the wounds of a man who had just been in an auto accident. There was a painted gash about the victim's eye and pretend-complaints about pain in the rib cage. So the actor-doctor proceeded to check him over.

My mouth probably came open in amazement at the awkward and stiff movements of the soap opera doctor. He touched the other man's eye with the finesse of a jack hammer operator and literally jabbed his ribs with rigid fingers at a 90-degree angle. The scene had a comic rather than a dramatic impact.

The hands of a real physician are incredibly gentle. They examine and treat painful areas of a patient's body with keen awareness of the person's distress and with concern not to add to or enlarge his pain. When those hands do cause pain, it is only to diagnose or perform a therapeutic function.

A physician's hands touch sensitive areas with keen awareness of one's pain and with concern not to add to it.

When Jesus dealt with sinners, there was never a clumsy touch to his deeds. Whether dealing with a woman caught in adultery or Peter's three denials, there was an impressive gentleness about him.

People who are filled with the Spirit of Christ exhibit his ability to heal rather than harm by their touch. If a fellow believer errs from the way of holy living, they know how to "restore him gently" (Gal. 6:1). If another espouses some false doctrine, they refuse painful quarreling and choose instead to "gently instruct" him in the healing truth (2 Tim. 2:24-26).

Too often we show ourselves to be destroyers rather than healers by our approach to sin. We hack, slash, and jab. We are clumsy, rigid, and hurtful. We get angry with the sinner rather than Satan in whose clutches the sinner is held. We pour salt rather than oil into wounds. Where did we learn such a method?

Then we are confused and angry when the world looks at the church and calls us "hypocrites." How could they think us hypocrites when all we are doing is opposing error and sin?

Maybe it has to do with our touch. I know the fellow on TV was an actor because of this clumsy manner. The Greek word for a person assuming a role different from his true nature is *hypokrites* (hypocrite = actor). Maybe the world has occasionally witnessed and felt too heavy a hand when the gentleness of Jesus' touch from us would have had a healthier effect.

The Healer's Touch

There is an amazing power in the physical act of touching another human being. As a matter of fact, touching is probably the most basic means we have to communicate with one another. At the very least, a touch is one person's way of saying to another, "You're not alone."

Seven-week old Ashley had been crying for half an hour. Her young, inexperienced mother patted her back, jostled her crib, and tried to put a pacifier in her mouth. Finally she picked her up, kissed her, and held her close. As tears of frustration flowed down her mother's cheeks, Ashley's stopped.

Almost 50 years ago, researchers discovered that babies in institutional care who were seldom held were sick oftener and grew at a slower rate than children who were caressed and touched. The mortality rate for those children was significantly higher. Healthy food. Good medical care. But too little contact with warm-blooded creatures.

Did you ever notice in the Gospels how Jesus made it a point to touch people? He made clay and put in on the eyes of the blind man. He took Jairus' daughter by the hand. He held babies in his arms. He put his hands on a woman who had been crippled for 18 years.

Furthermore, he let people touch him. No unlisted phone. No bodyguards. No "professional distance" from his disciples. He even let a prostitute wash his feet with her tears and dry them with her hair. Matthew tells about a day in Jesus' ministry when "all who touched him were healed."

Touching is one person's way of saying to another, "You're not alone."

Brad hadn't made it home for a Thanksgiving holiday for seven years. He had been something of the family's black sheep, and he had only recently gone through a drug rehabilitation program. He didn't know how he would be received, but he knew last year that he wanted to go home. At the front door, he put out his hand to his father. When his father took his hand, gently pulled him forward, and hugged him, he knew things were going to go well.

Natural, nonsexual, nonmiraculous "laying on of hands" is powerful communication. Without words, it affirms. Closes distance. Soothes human hurts. Gives security.

All of us complain at certain times about our inability with words. When there has been a major disappointment. A terrible diagnosis. A failure. Death. Maybe there is something better to do than talk.

Just be there. With a touch. A hug. Given with love, it is a healing touch in the spirit of the Great Physician.

He Needed
to Be Loved

If you're a sports fan, you may know the story already. If you're not a sports fan, you still need to know it. For the point of the story is not basketball. It is about the need we all have for security. Acceptance. Love. Family.

There was a little ten-year-old boy roaming the streets of Boston. He was homeless and hungry. His father had died in his native Jamaica, and his mother had turned him out of her house and life. She didn't want him.

Everything the boy owned was stuffed in a duffel bag. He scrounged for food. He slept in the hallways of buildings to stay dry and warm. He traipsed the streets during the daylight hours. "There were times when I used to cry," he would later recall, "wondering if I had a real mother."

Louis and Helen Ford stumbled across that homeless child one day. They took him to their house. They fed him all the pork chops, string beans, and potatoes he could get down. They put him in a real bed.

The next morning, he bounded down the stairs into the kitchen. He saluted Mrs. Ford with his best "Hi, Mom!" A family that already had five children decided it had a place for the sixth.

"There were times when I used to cry," he would recall, "wondering if I had a real mother."

The little boy was a gifted athlete. When he got into high school, he was a basketball star. It got him a scholarship to college. In January of 1989, he was in one of those clutch situations little boys fantasize while shooting hoops on the playground. With his team trailing by a single point with only seven seconds left, he was fouled. He had two free throws coming. He stepped up to the line. He missed the first. He missed the second. His team lost.

But he still had what he needed most in life. He still had his family. His mother still loved him. He would be all right, because he had a home.

Oh, yes. The same young man was in a similar situation on April 3, 1989. With his team trailing by one point and with three seconds left in overtime, he was fouled. This time it was a one-and-one situation. The opposing team called a timeout before he shot in order to put on more pressure.

Then Rumeal Robinson stepped to the line. The national championship at stake for Michigan against Seton Hall. Forty thousand fans were on their feet, and millions more were watching on television. He sank them both. He scored the winning points in one of the most dramatic college basketball games ever played. Every basketball player's fantasy had come true for one of the few people who will ever know the experience in reality.

I was watching the game on TV, and the camera went immediately from the jubilation on the court to two people in the stands. Louis and Helen Ford. Mrs. Ford, wearing a sweatshirt which said "Rumeal's Mom," was jumping up and down. You could read her lips. "Thank you, Jesus!" she said. "Thank you, Jesus!"

Thank *you*, Mr. and Mrs. Ford, for being heaven's angels to accept and love a child who had been rejected. For giving him refuge. For letting him have the chance to do something spectacular. For providing him a family.

Thank you for reminding us again of the power love has to heal our wounds and make us whole.

Is There Anything More to Say?

In the earlier part of the century, it was a custom for preachers after they had spoken to open the floor for comments from the audience. Questions could be asked. Clarification could be sought. Communication could be enhanced.

Such a procedure is also pregnant with risk. There was always the possibility that someone might take advantage of the situation to sound off, take the preacher to task, or push some pet theory. These facts of risk are likely what put an end to the practice!

At the end of one of his sermons, T. B. Larimore opened the floor for discussion. An angry man jumped to his feet and began challenging him on some point in his lesson. He stood and spoke for something over a quarter of an hour.

If you had been in his place, what might you have done? Knowing how defensive some of us are, we might have been tempted to respond point by point and try to turn the argument on him. Most of us probably would not have allowed him to keep the floor for 20 minutes. At the least, we could have responded in righteous indignation about such unprincipled behavior.

When the diatribe ended, Larimore spoke. "Thank you, sir," he said. "Does anyone else have something you would like to say?"

When no one in the stunned audience offered anything else, he turned back to the man who had maligned him and said, "Sir, would you lead us now in a closing prayer?"

We are never more tempted to lose control than in the face of personal attack.

It calls for tremendous self-control to take abusive treatment from another without responding in kind. Since self-control is a feature of the fruit of the Spirit, our general inability to withstand provocation surely testifies to the weakness of his presence in us. The weakness is not with him but relates to our degree of yieldedness to his transforming power.

Because Christ is in us, we do not have to be out-of-control people. We do not have to be victims of our temperaments, desires, or circumstances. We have the potential for self-control (i.e., temperance, moderation) in all things.

We are never more tempted to lose control than in the face of personal attack. Jesus knows what it is like. He not only had to bear with false accusations throughout his ministry but eventually with blows to his person. Although he could have struck back, he surprised both friend and foe by his restraint.

The ability to turn the other cheek is not weakness but spiritual exercise in self-discipline and Christlikeness. It is the response only love can generate.

Freedom Needs Love's Direction

"You, my brothers, were called to be free" (Gal. 5:13a).

Recently I watched a news story which both confused and angered me. It was about some Russian families who were leaving the United States after five years in our country. The confusion came from my initial amazement that anyone would choose to leave our free society for a totalitarian society. And the anger was a knee-jerk reaction to their rejection of American freedom.

I sat down, listened to the details of the story, and have not been able to get it out of my mind since. The emigres from Russia explained that they could not understand and cope with the freedom they were expected to exercise here. It had been too much for them to take control over their lives after growing up in a culture which had made all their decisions for them. Where to live, how much schooling your children get, what sort of work you will do and where you will do it are all decisions made for you by the state in the Soviet Union.

How do you react? Sound foolish to you? Think a bit longer, and I think it will both make sense and help explain some phenomena we have witnessed in our own culture. Here are some examples of what I have in mind:

> The theological revolution at the turn of the twentieth century effectively abolished Scripture as authority in religion. A rush to embrace theological liberalism created a host of placid pulpits and dying denominations.
>
> The social revolution of the '60s gave unprecedented freedom to a generation. "Fun" at any cost became the mandate. That spirit became the basis for a selfish, sometimes obscene, and often drug-intoxicated subculture.
>
> The sexual revolution of the '70s convinced us it was right for everyone to "have it all." Doing just that, teen pregnancies have soared, abortions have skyrocketed, and sexual diseases (including AIDS) have infected and are killing thousands.

"But do not use your freedom to indulge the sinful nature" (Gal. 5:13b).

All three of these revolutions were reactions to bad situations. The first was a pendulum-swing reaction to rigid legalism; the second was a rejection of social hypocrisies which enforced rules which had no rational justification (e.g., segregation); the third came about in response to prudish sexual attitudes, double standards for males and females, and too many marriages which children knew were held together by duty or guilt rather than love.

Knowing the penchant of human nature to go from one extreme to another, the obvious danger is that we will witness a swing back to the extreme right. A few years ago, there were some evidences that such a thing was afoot. There were extreme, dogmatic, and legalistic religious cults like the Jim Jones group which had inordinate influence; some right-wing political personalities (e.g., Lyndon LaRouche) and movements (e.g., Ku Klux Klan) were influencing elections and public policies; and some of the suggestions we have heard for dealing with the AIDS crisis sound positively medieval.

Some people are unable to cope with the freedom they are expected to exercise.

"Rather, serve one another in love" (Gal. 5:13c).
There is a Christian alternative to the evils of slavery versus self-destruction, right-wing conservatism versus left-wing liberalism, and legalism versus license.

Christ has set us free from legalistic codes and human traditions. But his freedom is the freedom to glorify God and serve others through love rather than by mere constraint of law. The life we are called to live is made possible by the indwelling of the Spirit of God rather than conformity to rules (cf. Gal. 5:16-18).

Christian freedom is a responsible freedom which does not flaunt itself as a ruse for fulfilling the desire of sinful human nature (cf. Gal. 5:19-21).

Christian freedom is a positive freedom. It is the freedom to be happy, to exercise voluntary self-control, to be patient with provocation, and so on. It is the freedom to be made like Christ by keeping in step with the Spirit's guidance (Gal. 5:22-25).

Freedom is hard to handle by people who have never known it before or who are so immature as to interpret it as the right to unrestrained indulgence. Like Russian emigres turning their backs on America, the inability of some Christians to handle freedom explains some of the apostasies from Christ we witness. Unable to understand and live in freedom, they return to the bondage of the world. People struggling with this issue need gentle guidance by older, more mature saints who have learned the meaning of being free men and women in Christ.

For all the dangers that come with freedom in Christ, the alternative of perpetual and hopeless bondage to Satan, wickedness, and human rules is far worse. And to those who learn to live in Christ's freedom by the power of the Holy Spirit to the glory of God the Father comes the fullness of eternal life.

Dear Father, help us to know the true meaning of the freedom you have given us in Christ. Having freed us from bondage, let us know the holy slavery of being free to love, serve, and glorify you in holiness. In Jesus' name we pray, Amen.

Using Religion to Hurt People

The Christian religion is intended to minister healing to people who are broken. Reading a passage from Isaiah one day, Jesus applied it to his work. That text speaks of good news to the poor, freedom for prisoners, sight for the blind, and release for the oppressed (Luke 4:16-21).

If the kingdom of heaven can be likened to a vineyard or field, it might also be likened to a hospital. Everyone in it is infected with the disease of sin, so no one can think himself better than any other. We are at various stages on the road to recovery, but we are all sinners. We are all being treated and healed by the same Great Physician.

God's presence once worked its healing wonders among sinners. During Jesus' personal ministry, he ate with sinners, made outcasts feel comfortable, and broke all manner of rabbinic rules in order to help people.

Nowadays it doesn't always work that way. The religion of Jesus sometimes winds up hurting people who have already been hurt too much.

It often isolates us from the world. Jesus went to the world, talked to the world, loved the world, and saved the world. Our church buildings and programs can get in the way of our mission unless we are careful.

The religion of Jesus Christ sometimes winds up hurting people who have already been hurt too much.

It can be used to insulate us from pain. Jesus took the pains of others to himself and bore their burdens. Are we to protect ourselves from similar sorrows? If we serve our Lord in this world, it will have to be through ministering to one of his least brothers.

It sometimes creates a sense of greater guilt rather than relief. Tax collectors and prostitutes left the presence of Jesus unburdened. Guilty, penitent people sometimes come to us only to be scolded, censured, and made to feel worse.

In our struggle to recapture the original essence of the Christian religion, we haven't always succeeded. Or, perhaps better stated, we have generally done better with doctrine than practice, better with law than spirit.

As part of the test we must apply to interpretation, practice, and corporate life, we must take account of the impact we have on people. For while it is false to think that whatever works is true, it is equally false to believe that something can be true which doesn't work.

Enough bashing, hurting, and destroying people in the name of Jesus! It's time for the healing to begin.

"Jesus, I Love You. Really. But . . ."

One day a believer came before the Lord to talk with him. He said:

"Lord Jesus, there are some matters we've needed to sort out for a long time. It keeps nagging at me that we are working at opposite purposes, so perhaps we need to talk. Clear the air. Lay all our cards on the table.

"Jesus, I love you but have to seek my own fulfillment rather than your kingdom when the two are in conflict. It's just human nature. After all, you made me the way I am.

For in my inner being I delight in God's law; but I see another law at work in the members of my body, waging war against the law of my mind and making me a prisoner of the law of sin at work within my members (Rom. 7:22-23).

"I love you, Jesus, but must hold on to my friends. Even the ones who cannot bring me closer to you and who often tempt me to sin against you. You surely understand about my need to be accepted by my peers.

"You know, Jesus, that I love you with my whole heart. But I can't think you want me to sacrifice money, prestige, or comfort. Even though they are most often for my glory than for yours.

And everyone who has left houses or brothers or sisters or father of mother or children or fields for my sake will receive a hundred times as much and will inherit eternal life. But many who are first will be last, and many who are last will be first (Matt. 19:29-30).

Man's heart is deceitful above all things and beyond cure. Who can understand it?

"Jesus, I really do love you but sometimes have this overwhelming urge to get even with people who hurt me rather than turn the other cheek. It just doesn't seem fair to have to take that stuff from anybody.

"Lord, you know I love you. But my self-esteem gets such a boost from leading and dominating that I just can't feel right being a follower and a servant. After all, what would my colleagues think of me in such a self-effacing role? It just wouldn't be me.

We love because he first loved us. If anyone says, "I love God," yet hates his brother, he is a liar. For anyone who does not love his brother, whom he has seen, cannot love God, whom he has not seen (1 John 4:19-20).

"And, Jesus, I love you but am having a difficult time with lots of my neighbors. Even my Christian brothers and sisters. Some of them are rude and selfish. Others are hypocritical. Why, I have to wonder whether some of them even love you very much at all.

"This little talk we've had has made me feel a lot better. I think we probably understand each other better now. Any reaction from you?"

The heart is deceitful above all things and beyond cure. Who can understand it? (Jer. 17:9).

Jesus' eyes looked sadder than they had ever looked before. As they filled with tears, he said, "You've said all there is to say. Your position is clear. There's nothing I can add."

The two then went their separate ways. One walked away with a jaunty spring in his step. The other walked away slowly, as if he were carrying the weight of the world on his back.

Their paths never crossed again.

Not Meant to Be

The history of the world could well be told in terms of a litany of things which never should have happened. No, more than that. It can be told in terms of *things never meant to be.*

Eden was never meant for sin.
Adam and Eve were not intended for shame.
Angels were not created to bar paradise.

Eyes were never meant for darkness,
nor ears fashioned for the sake of silence,
nor hearts created to be cold.

Birth was never meant to be a rendezvous with woe.
Life was not given for the sake of melancholy.
And death was not supposed to terrorize.

Love was never meant for indifference,
>nor truth and insight for unbelief,
>>nor offers of grace for rejection.

Animal feeding troughs were never meant to be
>cradles.
>Thorns are not suitable materials for a crown.
>Nails should never be driven through flesh.

The story is *scandalous* from start to finish. There is more disappointment than delight. There is more grief than joy. There is foolishness where we would expect to see wisdom, weakness where we look for strength.

The history of the world can be told in terms of a litany of things which were never meant to be.

Why would God stoop to function in such an arena? There is no logic to it, and everything about our natural sentiment warns against identifying with the cross. Why, it is the ultimate outrage to the human race.

But there it stands: *the cross*. There he stands: *Jesus Christ*. His offer of pardon by means of his own blood transforms folly to wonder. Sinners to saints. Death to life.

It is a miracle of love which God alone can perform.